The Comeback Guide

For Entrepreneurs

5 Steps for Turning Setbacks into Success

By
Steven Schain

This book has been gifted to:

_____

Important information about this book

This book provides specific methods and information used to recover from my business failure. Your situation is unique. Laws vary by state and change over time. Your situation may require personalized advice. What worked for me may need adjustment for you.

Get professional help when you need it. Consult qualified advisors for legal matters, financial planning, tax strategies, and other professional concerns. This book is not a replacement for professional legal advice, financial advice, or professional consultation.

While care was taken when preparing this book, I am human; there may be errors or missed details. I cannot guarantee perfect accuracy. There are no guaranteed results from following this advice. The strategies in this book will not work in every situation.

You make the final decisions. Use this book as a guide. Adapt the strategies to fit your needs. Seek professional help when required. Your recovery is your responsibility.

Copyright © 2025 by Steven Schain, The 3D Professor, LLC DBA AI Performance Partners
Cover design by Steven Schain
Cover Copyright © 2025 by Steven Schain, The 3D Professor, LLC DBA AI Performance Partners

All Rights Reserved

No part of this book may be reproduced, stored in a retrieval system, or transmitted by any means, electronic or mechanical, including photocopying, recording, or otherwise, without written permission from the copyright holder.

To learn more about this book and our growing community, visit **www.thecomebackguide.com**.

For April, my extraordinary partner in life

*"Between the business you closed
and the life you'll build lies a path.
This is your map."*
Steven Schain

Learn more and discover our growing community

Go to www.thecomebackguide.com
Become a member of
The Resilience Protocol Community
and start your journey today

Contents

Introduction 6

Part 1: The Fall 10

   Chapter 1: The Breaking Point 11

Part II: The 5 Steps to Recovery 21

   Chapter 2: Conduct an Honest Self-Assessment 22
   Chapter 3: Develop a Resilient Mindset 43
   Chapter 4: Set Clear, Achievable Goals 68
   Chapter 5: Create an Actionable Recovery Plan . 91
   Chapter 6: Build a Support Network 112

Part III: The New Beginning 130

   Chapter 7: Moving Forward with Confidence 131

Introduction

One year after my second business collapsed, I started another company.

Not because I'm reckless. Not because I'm a glutton for punishment. Because I discovered something during those brutal months of recovery: failure isn't the end of your entrepreneurial story. It's the beginning of your most important chapter.

The question is whether you have a system to write that chapter well.

Right now, you might be living through your worst professional nightmare. The business you poured your heart into is crashing. Maybe you've already closed the doors. Maybe bankruptcy papers sit on your desk. Every morning brings that familiar knot in your stomach. Every evening ends with questions that have no easy answers.

How did I get here? What will people think? Am I a complete failure?

These questions circle through your mind on repeat. You replay every decision, looking for the warning signs you missed. The financial loss hurts. The identity crisis cuts deeper. When being a business owner defines who you are, losing that business feels like losing yourself.

Here's what nobody tells you: You are not broken. You're experiencing something that successful entrepreneurs rarely talk about publicly. Business schools don't teach recovery strategies. Society celebrates wins and stays silent about comebacks. You're left to figure out rebuilding on your own.

I've been exactly where you are. My second business collapsed despite years of effort and significant investment. The financial devastation was brutal. The personal failure cut deeper. I know the sleepless nights. I know the constant anxiety. I know the fear that everyone sees you as someone who couldn't make it.

During my recovery, I developed a five-step system that pulled me out of that darkness. I call it The Resilience Protocol. These steps guided me from devastation to an exciting new business. More importantly, they gave me something failure-proof: a framework for turning any setback into forward momentum.

Here's what you'll do in the first week: identify the three specific decisions that led to the collapse. Not in a shame spiral. In a clear-eyed assessment that shows you exactly what to do differently. You'll know which assumptions to abandon forever.

By month two, you'll have rebuilt your decision-making foundation. You'll stop second-guessing yourself. The mental fog begins to lift because you have a system for processing setbacks without being crushed by them.

Within six months, you'll see tangible progress toward a new beginning. Not because you forgot what happened. Because you extracted every lesson from your failure and built something stronger on that foundation.

The most successful entrepreneurs you admire have failed. Many have failed spectacularly, multiple times. What's the difference between those who stay down for good and those who rise again? The ones who rise again have a system that guides them through recovery, step by step.

You're about to learn that system.

The Resilience Protocol works through five interconnected steps:

Step 1: Conduct an Honest Self-Assessment: Discover exactly what went wrong and your role in it, so you stop carrying the same blind spots into your next venture.

Step 2: Develop a Resilient Mindset: Build mental tools that prevent one setback from destroying your confidence and keep you moving forward when everything feels impossible.

Step 3: Set Clear, Achievable Goals: Transform overwhelming chaos into specific, manageable targets that create momentum through small wins.

Step 4: Create an Actionable Recovery Plan: Turn vague hopes into a concrete roadmap with clear next steps you can take tomorrow.

Step 5: Build a Support Network: Stop facing this alone by assembling a team of people who understand where you've been and where you're going.

Each step builds on the previous one, creating a complete system for recovery.

This book shows you how to execute each step. No fluff. No empty promises. Practical strategies that work in the real world when everything feels like it's falling apart.

Right now, you feel defeated. Six months from now, you'll wake up energized about your future. You'll have rebuilt your confidence. You'll understand exactly what went wrong and how to prevent it from happening again. You'll be part of a community of entrepreneurs who've walked this same path and come out stronger. The question isn't whether you can recover; it's whether you'll take the first step today.

Here's what I know from working with dozens of entrepreneurs throughout the years: The ones who wait often stay stuck for years. They bounce from one half-started idea to another. They carry the same blind spots into their next venture. They never fully recover their confidence because they never had a system to process what happened. Six months becomes a year.

A year becomes three. The failure that could have been a turning point becomes a permanent weight they carry.

You'll see your setback as the beginning of your most important chapter. You'll develop skills that serve you in every future challenge. You'll discover strengths you didn't know existed.

Your failure doesn't define your future. Your response to failure does.

This difficult chapter is one chapter in a longer story. You're about to write what happens next, and this book shows you how to write it well.

Your recovery starts now.

Steven Schain

Part 1: The Fall

Chapter 1:
The Breaking Point

I know what it feels like to have your life come crashing down.

One day, I ran a growing business. The next day, I closed the doors. I was 57 when my 3D printing company, Spectra3D, shut down and I declared bankruptcy. It felt like everything ended. The financial loss hurt, but the personal failure cut deeper.

I remember walking into Spectra3D's workshop, with 3D printers humming day and night. To meet the high demand, we had more than 20 printers, each of which was churning out a part for a client who eagerly awaited its delivery. We had a small team working on exciting new projects, and the future looked full of promise.

Then, one day, it got quiet. The equipment went unused. Every morning, I felt that familiar knot in the pit of my stomach and a familiar question came to my mind. Would today bring the miracle client who'd save us?

Deep down, I knew better.

The stress became too much. My optimism turned to denial. I ignored what the numbers, and my gut, clearly showed. Each morning, I'd look at our accounts, see the declining balance, then convince myself it was temporary. I'd create elaborate scenarios where a big client would call, or our new product line would suddenly take off. I made spreadsheets projecting growth that were not based on reality. Deep down, I knew these projections were a fantasy, but I couldn't face what they meant: my company was dying and needed to be closed.

By September 2023, I broke. I remember that day clearly. I'd spent hours poring over spreadsheets, looking at empty bank accounts, and making excuses for the non-existent paychecks. Once again, I walked through the door at home, completely drained, filled with stress, and feeling defeated. I dropped onto the couch without even taking off my shoes. That's when it hit me: the business I built was destroying my health. The anxiety I'd been ignoring flared like a warning shot—I couldn't keep living like this.

I knew it was the end, and I felt at my lowest.

But…

It also was the start of something new.

Maybe you're living this right now. Your business shut down or you lost your job. You're beginning to realize that your choices led you here. The shame keeps you up at night. The fear makes you avoid phone calls. The uncertainty makes every decision feel impossible.

You picked up this book because you need a way forward. Not platitudes about 'bouncing back.' Not inspirational quotes about failure building character. You need a proven system that works when everything feels broken.

You need The Resilience Protocol.

The first thing I need to tell you is, *you are not alone*.

I wrote this book not only to share my story with you but also to guide you through your recovery. Use this book and the accompanying workbooks as you start acting toward recovery.

The second thing I need to tell you is, *you are not your failure*.

I know it feels like it, but you're not. This book begins by exploring what failure is and what it means in your life. Only by understanding failure can you overcome it.

This is where my story—and yours—begins.

Failure and Denial

We Rarely Talk About Failure

We talk about success all the time. Stories of the latest achievements, championships, and triumphs are everywhere: on television, in magazines, and across thousands of websites. But we rarely talk about failure.

When your business fails, you lose a job, or a relationship ends, it feels like a personal failure. That failure brings shame, anxiety, fear, depression, and even isolation.

Yet, everyone fails. Even the most successful people have failed, often many times, before they succeeded. I can almost guarantee that, whether or not they admit it, inside every one of those success stories, there is at least one failure. The difference is what they did after failing.

Failure seldom happens all at once. Small defeats pile up over time. Each setback chips away at your confidence, resources, and resolve.

The company's troubles started in mid-2021, a little over a year into the COVID lockdown. After growing the company by more than 18% year over year, by the end of 2021, our revenue dropped by almost half. Our main clients, industrial metal casting companies, shut down and stopped production. Before its final shutdown in 2024, My company was known for high-quality 3D-printed casting patterns throughout the industry. In a matter of months, that market vanished.

I thought it was temporary. Many businesses struggled then. We needed to wait it out and soon, everything would return to normal. So, I took loans to stay afloat, hoping for that next job that would fix everything.

Each morning, I checked emails hoping for client inquiries. Each day without them felt like failure all over again. "Tomorrow will be different," I told myself. "Next week we'll get a big order." I stayed hopeful even as our bank account drained and debt grew.

That big job never came. I knew it wouldn't, and I couldn't admit it.

Warning Signs Missed

I couldn't see clearly because I was too close to my business. However, the red flags were everywhere:

- Bills were higher than income.
- Global competitors offered cheaper services.
- New markets didn't bring enough money.

- Stress got worse every day.
- Personal funds and loans propped up the business.

Looking back, the financial warning signs were obvious. Every month, expenses exceeded revenue. But instead of addressing the core problem, I'd scramble for quick fixes - more loans, retirement withdrawals, new credit cards.

The market was changing too. Our competitors could produce similar work at lower costs, and our target industries started to bring 3D printing in-house. While I acknowledged this reality, I kept telling myself our quality was better, and our service more personal. However, clients increasingly chose larger printing services, with similar costs but much higher capacity and material options. One long-time customer called to say they were moving their business away from 3D printing in the US to injection molding overseas. "Just a business decision," they said. I understood their reasoning. I saw that bright red flag. But knowing exactly what it meant didn't change how I ran the business.

Every day, I told myself these were temporary problems. We needed one big client or one good product launch. Our Etsy shop would take off. Our new jigs and fixtures division would find its footing, or our golf product would sell thousands of units. I call this "hope as a strategy." It doesn't work. Hope keeps you going, but without concrete changes and realistic assessment, it simply delays the inevitable. I wasted months hoping instead of adapting or preparing for the end.

The Physical and Emotional Toll

My health deteriorated in scary ways. As a heart attack survivor, I knew stress was dangerous; my cardiologist had warned me it was "as dangerous as smoking." But I kept stress-eating, working through lunch, and coming home too wound up to sleep. My blood pressure spiked, requiring new medication. The business wasn't only failing financially - it was destroying my body.

Nights were the worst. I'd jolt awake in the middle of the night, calculating how long we could last without a new client. Every unpaid bill haunted me. My body started sending clearer signals—

the persistent neck pain from the stress, the upset stomach that no amount of antacids could help.

During that time, I'd gone on autopilot. When I finally closed the shop, the stress stuck around for a while. I still woke up panicking about what to do. I still felt my stomach drop when I thought about the next steps. But, little by little, something shifted. I started sleeping better and taking care of myself physically, mentally, and emotionally. Each day got a little easier. Gradually, I stopped seeing the end of my business as a failure. Maybe, it was the end of a chapter.

The Cost of Denial

Denial is expensive in terms of money, emotions, and health:

- By closing time, I had nearly three times the debt I would have had one year earlier.
- Each extra month meant more bills, unpaid invoices, and stress.
- I became irritable and distant from people I cared about.
- I pretended everything was fine because I couldn't face telling the truth.
- As a heart attack survivor, I knew stress could kill me.
- I wasted time I could have spent healing and building something new.

The financial hit was brutal. I remember looking at my books when I tallied the final numbers. "If I had closed only a year ago," I told myself, "I'd be looking at less than half of this debt and I'd have money in my bank account." I stared at the figure: $354,000 in business debt that partially became personal debt through my guarantees and loans. That doesn't include the more than $200,000 I pulled from personal savings or the money from my retirement account and the sale of my stocks. All gone, not invested in something new, not saved for my future. Gone, burned trying to save a business that was already dead.

I kept telling vendors "The money is coming," hoping there was a miracle around the corner. I stopped answering calls from numbers I didn't recognize. My once-pristine credit score dropped. I'll be rebuilding my financial life for years because I couldn't face reality.

The denial cost me more than money. It cost me health, relationships, and time I could have used to process what happened and build something sustainable.

What is your denial costing you? Be brutally honest about what you're paying in money, relationships, health, and missed opportunities. Make a list with two columns: what you're gaining by continuing down your current path, and what it's costing you. When I finally did this exercise, my "gain" column had one item: "Avoid the shame of admitting failure." My "cost" column filled the page.

The Value of Taking Downtime

For business owners, your company becomes part of you. Every success feels personal. Every failure cuts deep. I had been "the owner of Spectra3D" so long I couldn't imagine being anyone else. Saying "I used to own a business" felt like admitting defeat.

After deciding to close the business, I felt mixed emotions. I grieved for what could have been, the growth, innovations, and the team. But I also felt relief, like putting down a heavy weight. For months, I had carried a failing business, pretending everything was fine. Being honest with myself was the first step toward my new life.

Taking time to heal before jumping into what was next wasn't wasted time. It was essential.

Many people rush from failure straight into the next venture, carrying their unprocessed emotions and old patterns with them.

I nearly made this mistake too. The pressure to bounce back immediately is strong. We worry about gaps in our résumés or what others might think if we're not visibly productive.

Instead, I allowed myself a period of rest and reflection. During this time:

- My body began to heal from stress.
- I reconnected with friends and family.
- I permitted myself to grieve the loss.
- I gained perspective on what went wrong.
- I discovered what truly mattered to me.

This downtime wasn't about giving up. It was about creating space to process what happened so I could move forward with clarity instead of desperation. It allowed me to break patterns that might have led me straight into another failure.

How much downtime you need depends on your situation. For some, it might be weeks, for others, months. The key is to use this time intentionally, not only to recover, but also to reflect and realign.

Ask yourself: Have you given yourself time to heal from your setback? Or are you rushing to the next thing to avoid facing your feelings?

Breaking Free from the Success—Failure Trap

Here's a key insight from my recovery: success and failure aren't opposites. They're two parts of the same journey. Many see life as winning or losing. Reality, however, isn't so black and white. It's messier. I learned the hard way that wins and losses are stepping stones along the path of a good life. For months, I called myself "a failed business owner." I saw bankruptcy as proof I wasn't as good as others. This mindset kept me stuck.

Shifting out of those thoughts came slowly, but eventually, I stopped seeing myself as someone who failed and instead as someone who had experienced failure, learned from it, and moved forward. This small language change reflected a huge mindset shift. My worst moment didn't define me. It allowed me to respond and learn from it.

How do you talk about your failure? Do you say, "I am a failure," or "I experienced a failure"? This small difference dramatically affects your ability to move forward.

A Roadmap for Turning Failure into a Fresh Start

Failure isn't the end; it's a turning point. If you're facing a setback, you can decide what comes next.

Through my recovery journey and conversations with others who've faced similar challenges, I've developed a five-step system I call **The Resilience Protocol**. It's the exact framework I used to move from devastation to a new beginning. Here's how it works:

Conduct an Honest Self-Assessment
Accept what happened without blame. Let yourself feel upset and know that recovery takes time. Write down what you've learned and how to use it. Be specific about what went wrong and what you'd change.

Develop a Resilient Mindset
Learn to bounce back from setbacks with strategies that build mental resilience. Change how you talk to yourself about failure. Develop habits that strengthen your ability to persist through challenges.

Set Clear, Achievable Goals
Create specific, meaningful targets aligned with your true values. Set short-term goals you can achieve quickly to build momentum. Use SMART goals: specific, measurable, attainable, relevant, and time-bound.

Create an Actionable Recovery Plan
Build a practical roadmap that turns your goals into daily actions. Break down big goals into small steps you can take consistently. Create systems that help you stay on track even when motivation fluctuates.

Build a Support Network
Surround yourself with people who will help you grow through this challenge. Find mentors who've overcome similar setbacks. Create routines that strengthen these connections. You might be surprised how many people have faced this same thing and don't talk about it.

These aren't theoretical steps. They're exactly how I rebuilt my life. They come from difficult experiences, talking with others who faced similar problems, and proven recovery methods. The next five chapters of this book will guide you through these five steps in detail. Use the companion workbook through each step to document your personal journey. You can access the workbook at **www.thecomebackguide.com**

Recovery Happens Through Daily Habits

Recovery happens through daily habits that rebuild your life incrementally. Routines that helped me:

- **Morning talks:** My wife and I created "Couch Time," sitting with coffee or tea and talking. This simple ritual helped us connect and support each other.

- **Physical health:** Regular gym visits and better eating helped restore my energy and mental clarity.

- **Mindset work:** I listened regularly to The Mindset Mentor podcast by Rob Dial, which helped shift my perspective.
- **Reflection time:** Noticing small progress helped me see I was moving forward, even slowly.

Find routines that work for you. The goal is to build stability and momentum while working on bigger changes.

Your Next Chapter Starts Now

Your recovery doesn't happen in isolation. The entrepreneurs who rebuild fastest do three things: they get clear on what happened (you'll do this in Chapter 2), they build mental resilience (Chapter 3), and they join a community of others on the same path.

Go to www.thecomebackguide.com and download the free assessment workbook and learn more about The Resilience Protocol Community. It'll help you work through your recovery process and is the catalyst for your personal comeback story.

Your next chapter is waiting. Take the first step now.

Part II: The 5 Steps to Recovery

Chapter 2: Conduct an Honest Self-Assessment

The Mirror Moment

Sitting alone at my desk one morning, I stared at spreadsheets that showed the truth. The numbers didn't lie. My business was failing. I'd spent months avoiding this moment, creating stories about the big client who would save us or the product that would take off.

Shame and despair washed over me in waves. Fear followed close behind. What would I tell my wife? My one employee who had helped build the company and had been with me for years? My friends who saw me as successful?

The thoughts hit me rapidly: "Why did I ignore the signs?" "The evidence was right in front of me for years." "Everyone will know I failed." "What if I can't find a job after this?" "What will bankruptcy do to my future?" "I've wasted all those years."

That morning, I finally asked myself the questions I'd been dodging: What happened? What part did I play in this failure? What patterns led me here?

The answers hurt. I found that I had ignored warning signs, made poor financial choices, and let my ego drive business decisions, without a good plan. Most painful was seeing how I had tied my identity to my business success.

When I got home from the office that day, I told my wife everything. She helped me see the truth I had been hiding from. Our conversation opened my eyes. I realized then that I needed to close the business. She understood it would be difficult.

After our talk, I made three decisions:

1. Stop pretending things were fine.
2. Close the business within 3 months.
3. Start working on a shutdown plan.

It took me more than a week to create the plan for closing the business. It took me even longer to complete my honest self-assessment. However, it was my first real step toward recovery. Without it, I would have carried the same blind spots into my next venture.

Why We Avoid Self-Assessment

Most of us skip this step after failure. We rush to move on, to make ourselves feel better, to find the next job, or even to start a new business. We avoid examining our failures because it's difficult, and because we want to escape the pain of looking at our mistakes.

I did this after my first business setback years ago. I jumped straight into a new job without asking what went wrong. However, avoiding self-assessment meant that I carried the same problems forward.

Common avoidance tactics include:

- Blaming outside forces entirely.
- Jumping into the next project too quickly.
- Focusing only on financial losses.
- Telling yourself, "I'll think about it later."
- Dwelling on regrets without analyzing patterns.

Why do we avoid looking inward? Self-assessment hurts. It makes us face our weaknesses, poor choices, and missed opportunities. It's easier to blame the economy, competitors, or bad luck. It's harder to blame ourselves.

The human brain tries to protect us from pain. When we fail, our brain builds defense mechanisms:

- Denial: "The business isn't really failing."

- Selective memory: "We had a great first three years" (ignoring the bad years).
- External blame: "The market crashed" (ignoring our poor planning).
- Distraction: Keeping busy so we don't have to think about it.

I used all of these defenses. For months, I denied the reality of my situation. I focused on past successes while ignoring current problems. I blamed the pandemic shutdown for all of my troubles.

These defenses might protect your ego in the short term. However, they block the learning that helps you to grow.

True growth comes from asking hard questions:

- Which choices did I make that led here?
- Which warnings did I ignore?
- Which patterns keep showing up in my life?
- What will I do differently next time?

These questions feel uncomfortable. They should. Growth happens at the edge of your comfort zone.

Quiz: Honest Self-Assessment

Rate yourself on these statements from 1 (not at all) to 5 (completely):

1. ___**I understand exactly why my business/career experienced problems.**
   This measures your clarity about root causes, not just symptoms. Many people know their business failed but can't pinpoint exactly why.

2. ___**I can name specific mistakes I made without blaming others.**

   This tests your ability to take responsibility. Can you list your errors without adding, "but the economy also..." or, "my business partner should have..."?

3. ___**I recognize patterns in my decision making that contributed.**

   This reveals whether you see the bigger picture. One bad choice might be bad luck. Repeated bad choices reveal a pattern.

4. __**I've identified skills I need to develop.**

   This shows self-awareness about your limitations. Which specific abilities would have helped you to succeed?

5. __**I understand how my personal values affected my choices.**

   This explores the connection between who you are and how you operated. Did your need for approval, fear of conflict, or other values drive poor decisions?

Calculate your score:_____

What your score means:

- **5 – 10:** You're still in denial. This chapter will help you break through.
- **11 – 15:** You've started the process but need to dig deeper.
- **16 – 20:** You have good awareness but can sharpen your insights.
- **21 – 25:** You've done serious reflection. Use this chapter to fill any gaps.

My first score was a lowly 7. I understood surface problems but hadn't connected them to my patterns and values.

When I took this quiz again after honest reflection, I scored 18. I had clarity about what went wrong and my role in it.

Four Areas of Self-Assessment

Self-assessment helps you know where you stand before moving forward. This goes beyond listing what went wrong. You create a clear picture of your current situation, strengths, weaknesses, and lessons learned.

The process covers four key areas of your life: financial, skills, relationships, and values. For true recovery, take your time creating an honest picture of where you are now in these areas. This will form the foundation for all of the steps that follow.

1. Financial Assessment

Start with the numbers. They tell a clear story without emotion. Financial data doesn't lie, hide, or sugarcoat. While we may avoid looking at our bank account or create mental justifications, the numbers reveal the unvarnished truth about our situation.

Many business owners, myself included, develop an emotional relationship with their business. We see what we want to see. We focus on the big sale from last month rather than the six months of losses beforehand. Numbers cut through this emotional fog. They show patterns that otherwise might be missed and reveal problems that were being ignored.

When I finally sat down with my complete financial records, the story they told was uncomfortable but undeniable. The downward trend wasn't a temporary setback, but rather, a clear trajectory showing consistent decline. The financial assessment was the coldest, hardest part of my self-evaluation, but also the most clarifying.

I remember the morning I finally did it. I poured a cup of coffee, sat down at my desk, and opened the final year's spreadsheets. The screen showed a sea of red; the numbers felt like a physical punch. Every cell was a monument to a bad decision or a moment of denial. My first instinct was to stand up and walk away. But I forced myself to sit there, to look at the unvarnished truth. And as time ticked by, a strange thing happened. The panic started to subside, replaced by a cold, hard clarity. The dreaded task I'd been avoiding for months wasn't a vague idea anymore. It had a number, and a shape. For the first time, I wasn't fighting a ghost; I was facing an enemy I could see.

Look at your finances during the past 1 – 3 years:

- Month-by-month income
- All expenses
- Cash-flow patterns
- Debt accumulation
- Changes in profit margins

Ask yourself:

- When did the numbers first show problems?
- Which financial decisions made things worse?
- Where did I waste money?
- What expenses could I have cut sooner?

I'd burned all my money trying to save a business that hadn't been profitable for years, in the hope that I could make it back. Plus, I kept taking loans when it was clear that the core business model was broken.

I found these specific mistakes:

- I increased the spending on new equipment when sales were down and we didn't need the equipment.
- I waited too long to cut unnecessary expenses.
- I used credit cards for business costs at high interest rates.
- I ignored the declining profit margins on our main services.

Your financial assessment will likely feel painful. That's good. The pain shows you what not to repeat.

Five Key Financial Metrics to Review

Focus on these five numbers during your assessment:

1. **Monthly Burn Rate**: How much cash your business used each month. Many owners track revenue but not their burn rate. I was shocked to find that my business burned more than $20,000 monthly in its final year with only two employees.
2. **Debt-to-Income Ratio**: Total debt payments divided by monthly income. Mine reached well over 70%, far above the 36% safety threshold that financial experts recommend.
3. **Cash Runway**: How many months could you survive with no new income? My runway shrank from 6 months to 2 weeks without me noticing.
4. **Customer Acquisition Cost**: The amount you spend bringing in each new customer. Mine increased from around $50 to roughly $900, while customer value stayed flat and even began to decline.
5. **Profit Margins by Product/Service**: Which offerings made money? I discovered our main service had been making a much lower profit margin than I originally planned. Even though it looked like we were bringing in cash, we were losing money on most jobs.

These metrics reveal your true financial health. When I finally looked at them honestly, I saw I had been losing money, and that the business was propped up only by my financial support and loans.

Red Flag Financial Patterns

Watch for these danger signs:

- Using personal funds to cover business expenses more than twice in six months
- Paying only the minimum amount on business debts
- Delaying payments to suppliers and vendors

- Taking new loans to pay old debts
- Making financial decisions based on hope rather than data
- Avoiding looking at financial statements

I experienced all six red flags but ignored them. Don't make the same mistake.

Time to Face Financial Facts

1. Pull out your financial statements from the past year.
2. Mark the point where problems first appeared.
3. Identify three financial decisions that you regret.
4. Write down what you'll do differently next time.
5. Calculate your five key financial metrics right now.

2. Skills Assessment

Next, take an honest look at your skills. This requires a level of self-awareness that can be uncomfortable. Many entrepreneurs believe they're good at everything. Or should be. I certainly did. But this mindset prevents us from recognizing critical skill gaps that may have contributed to our failure.

Conducting a skills assessment means setting aside your ego. It means acknowledging that being talented in some areas doesn't make you competent in all areas. When my business was failing, I had to admit that while I excelled at product development and design, I was terrible at financial planning and marketing strategy.

This assessment isn't about beating yourself up. It's about creating an accurate map of your abilities. Think of it like taking inventory of tools in your workshop. Some tools are shiny and well-used. Others are rusty or missing entirely. You need to know what you have before you can build something new.

My ego did not like this exercise. Not one bit. In my head, I was the '3D printing guy,' the 'technical guru.' But when I was forced to list the skills I lacked that hurt my business, the list was brutally short and clear: 'Financial forecasting. Sales conversations. Saying no to unprofitable projects.' It was humbling to admit that the things I was worst at were the very things a CEO needs to be best at. It hurt. But it was also the most useful thing I'd done all year. It showed me exactly where the holes in my lifeboat were.

Make two lists:

1. Skills you have that helped your business.
2. Skills you lack that hurt your business.

Be specific. "Bad at marketing" is too vague. "Didn't understand how to set up Facebook ads" is specific.

My assessment revealed that I had strong technical skills but weak financial management abilities. I was good at making products but not at selling them profitably.

My skill gaps included:

- Financial forecasting
- Pricing strategy
- Sales conversations with new clients
- Cash-flow management
- Saying no to unprofitable projects

For each skill gap, ask:

- How did this hurt my business?
- Could I learn this skill?
- Should I partner with someone who has this skill?
- How will I address this gap next time?

Discover Your Skillset

3. Establish your five strongest business skills.
4. Identify five skills you lack that hurt your business.
5. For missing skills, write down whether to 'learn it,' 'hire it,' or 'partner' for it.
6. Choose one skill to start developing this month and learn it.

3. Relationship Assessment

No business or career exists in isolation. Assess how your relationship may have affected your situation. The people around you shape your decisions, provide support or present obstacles, and influence your thinking more than you might realize.

When businesses fail, we often focus on financial and strategic factors while overlooking the critical role that relationships play. My own failure assessment revealed that relationship dynamics contributed significantly to my downfall. I avoided difficult conversations with my employee about company finances. I attended industry meetups and events, thinking I would find the solution I needed. I kept my partner in the dark about the mounting debt until it was too late.

Relationship patterns can sabotage even the soundest business model. During stress, we tend to withdraw from the very people who could help us. We avoid mentors who might give tough feedback. We network to find superficial confirmation, when what we need most is honest connections. We hide problems from loved ones, depriving ourselves of crucial support.

The relationship assessment requires brutal honesty about both personal and professional connections. It means examining not only who was in your circle, but also how you interacted with them, what conversations you avoided, and what support you failed to seek. This examination reveals that it's often isolation, whether chosen or accidental, that accelerates your decline.

Look at these relationships:

- Business partners
- Employees
- Family members
- Mentors and advisors
- Customers and clients
- Vendors and suppliers

For each relationship, ask:

- How did this relationship help or hurt my business?

- What conversations did I avoid?
- Who did I listen to that I shouldn't have?
- Who should I have listened to but didn't?
- How did stress change my interactions?

I realized I had avoided talking to mentors who might have given difficult advice. I also saw how my stress had strained my relationship with my partner. I kept problems from my employee until it was too late.

My relationship patterns included:

- Avoiding difficult conversations about money
- Not seeking help when I needed it
- Becoming isolated when stressed
- Pretending everything was fine
- Not being honest with my partner about the business situation

Relationship Action Steps

1. Identify the five most important relationships in your work life.
2. Rate how each relationship helped or hurt your business.
3. Recognize one conversation you avoided but needed to have.
4. Determine how you'll handle similar situations in the future. Write it down.

4. Values Assessment

Finally, look at how your values align with your actions. This is the most profound part of self-assessment, yet it's the one most people skip. Misaligned values create a constant, energy-draining tension that undermines success, even when everything else seems right.

I spent years claiming I valued work-life balance while regularly working 12-hour days. I said family was my priority, but I missed important events for business meetings. I believed in transparent leadership, but I hid financial problems from my team. These contradictions created an internal conflict that affected my decision making and drained my resilience.

Values assessment requires looking beyond what you say is important to what your actions show is important. It's about confronting the gap between your stated principles and your reality. When I examined my calendar and bank statements, they told a different story about my values than the one I told myself.

The moment of truth for me wasn't in a spreadsheet; it was in a photograph of a concert I was supposed to attend. I wasn't in it. I had missed it for a 3D printing conference that, in hindsight, led to nothing. I had told myself and everyone else that my relationship was my number one value. But looking at that photo, I realized my calendar and credit card statements told the real story of my values, and it wasn't a story I was proud of. The business hadn't just taken my money; it had taken the time I could never get back. That was a cost far greater than any debt.

Many business failures stem from this disconnect. You might value creativity but force yourself into administrative roles. You might value authenticity but create a business that requires you to pretend. You might value security but take unsustainable risks. These contradictions create stress that eventually breaks even the strongest entrepreneur.

This assessment also reveals how much of yourself you've sacrificed to your business. I discovered I had compromised my health, relationships, and financial security—things I claimed were non-negotiable—all while telling myself I was making "necessary sacrifices for success."

Ask yourself:

- Which values drove my business decisions?
- Which values did I compromise?
- What matters most to me now?
- How did my identity get tied to my work?

Look for conflicts between:

- What you say is important
- How you spend time and money
- The choices you make under pressure

I discovered I had chased money and recognition at the expense of health and relationships. My definition of success needed to change.

My values assessment showed:

- I valued status more than I admitted.
- I compromised my health for work.
- I claimed to value work-life balance, but my work schedule showed otherwise.
- My identity was completely tied to being a "successful business owner."

This was my most painful assessment, but it led to the biggest changes in my life.

Determine Your Values

1. Identify five values you claim are important to you. Write them down.
2. Compare your calendar and bank statements—do they match your values?
3. Recognize five values you compromised for your business. Write them down.
4. Develop a new definition of success based on your true values. Write it down.

Creating Your Self-Assessment Map

Now, create a complete self-assessment map.

Step 1: Draw a timeline

Mark key events from the start of your business/job to its end. Include:

- Major decisions
- Warning signs
- Missed opportunities
- External events

Step 2: Circle decision points

Highlight moments where you made choices that shaped outcomes.

Step 3: Note patterns

Look for repeated behaviors or situations.

Step 4: Write your honest story

Write 1-2 pages about what happened. Include:

- Your role in the outcome
- What you learned
- How you've changed

Sample Self-Assessment Map

Here's part of my map:

Timeline

- Early 2016: Sold Spectralight Images training group; took full-time job.
- Mid-2016: Created Spectra3D for 3D printing; hired a manager.
- March 2020: COVID lockdown begins.
- Late 2020: First signs of client industry slowing.
- Early 2021: Main clients shut down production line.
- September 2021: Leave full-time job to work on the company.
- Late 2021: Revenue shows signs of significant decline; obtained loans.
- Early 2022: Branched out into new markets to increase revenue.
- Mid-2022: Created new product lines that didn't gain traction; obtained more loans.
- Early 2023: Stress from company issues threaten my health and relationships.
- September 2023: Decision made to close business and file for bankruptcy.

Key Patterns

- Ignored financial warning signs repeatedly
- Used hope instead of data to make decisions
- Didn't focus on core strengths

- Tied personal worth to business success
- Avoided difficult conversations

My Story

"I failed to face reality about my business and how I was running it. Even though we adapted when the market changed, I kept hoping things would return to normal. I took loans to buy time, rather than solve the core problem. My pride prevented me from admitting the business wasn't working until my health and relationships were suffering."

Moving Forward with Clarity

The purpose of self-assessment isn't to beat yourself up. It's to gain clarity so you don't repeat the same patterns. Think of this process as how pilots and aviation experts review flight data after an incident. They don't analyze what went wrong to assign blame, they do it to fly safer next time.

Many people avoid honest self-assessment because they fear it will confirm their worst thoughts about themselves: "I'm a failure," "I'm not cut out for business," or. "I don't have what it takes." But that's not what a proper assessment reveals. Instead, it shows specific behaviors and decisions that didn't serve you well; all things you *can* change.

During my self-assessment, I discovered patterns I'd been repeating for years. I saw how I consistently ignored financial warning signs. I noticed how I retreated from supportive relationships when times get tough. I didn't limit the focus of the business but tried to deliver too many products and services to too many markets. I recognized how I made decisions based on ego rather than data. These weren't character flaws, they were habits and blind spots I could address.

This clarity brings freedom. Instead of carrying vague shame about failure, you'll have concrete areas to work on. Rather than wondering if you're fundamentally flawed, you'll see specific skills to develop. In place of the fear that you'll fail again for mysterious reasons, you'll have a detailed map of the pitfalls you need to avoid.

Self-assessment transforms failure from a life sentence to a learning experience. It takes you from, "I am a failure" to, "That venture failed because of specific factors I now understand." This shift is not superficial; it's the difference between being crushed by failure or being educated by it.

After my assessment, I made four commitments:

1. Never again ignore financial warning signs.
2. Build my next career around my true values.
3. Focus my efforts on one task.
4. Separate my identity from my work.

These clear insights became the foundation for my recovery plan. Your self-assessment will reveal specific lessons that form the basis for the next steps in your journey.

Real Results: An Honest Assessment

After completing my self-assessment, I gained even more peace about my decision to close the business. I stopped seeing myself as a failure and started seeing myself as someone who made mistakes that I could learn from.

This clarity helped me to make better choices about what to do next. Instead of rushing into another venture with the same blind spots, I took time to build skills in areas where I was weak.

Chapter Summary

This chapter walks you through the first essential step of recovery from failure: conducting an honest self-assessment. You discover how true recovery starts when you face reality instead of hiding behind protective stories that keep you stuck. When you work through the four key areas: financial, skills, relationships, and values, you create a clear picture of what actually happened and your role in it.

You transform vague feelings of failure into specific, actionable insights through this assessment process. Instead of carrying the weight of being "a failure," you now understand exactly which behaviors and decisions didn't serve you well. This shift changes everything because you move from "I am broken" to "I made mistakes I can learn from." You turn the patterns you discovered into your roadmap to avoid the same pitfalls in your next chapter.

Remember that you don't use self-assessment to beat yourself up, you use it to create an accurate foundation for moving forward. You build every step that follows on the clarity you gain through this honest look at your situation. You can't build something better until you understand what went wrong, and now you do. This truth, while uncomfortable, sets you free to create the future you envision.

Share your insights with one trusted person who understands what you're going through. If you don't have someone in your life who's experienced business failure, The Resilience Protocol Community provides that crucial support.

When the community launches, founding members will share their self-assessment insights in our private forum. The feedback they receive reveals patterns they couldn't see on their own. The perspective from entrepreneurs who've done this work accelerates recovery in ways working alone cannot match.

Want to be among the founding members? Go to **www.thecomebackguide.com** and join the early access list.

This Week's Action Steps

1. Complete the four assessments (financial, skills, relationships, values).
2. Create your timeline and identify patterns.

3. Write your honest story without blame.
4. Share your insights with one trusted person.
5. Make three specific commitments based on what you learned.

Key Takeaways

- Self-assessment prevents repeating the same mistakes.
- Look at finances, skills, relationships, and values.
- Patterns matter more than individual mistakes.
- Your honest story becomes your foundation for growth.

Reflection Question

Did your business fail because you didn't like sales and avoided it, or because you didn't have the right management skillset? Or was there some other reason you can now identify?

This insight can lead you to uncover your patterns, learn from them, and grow.

Now that you know what happened, it's time to build the mental foundation for your comeback. That foundation starts with resilience; the mental armor you'll build in the next chapter.

A Note About Community"
The exercises in this chapter work. I used them myself. But they work better when you're surrounded by people doing them with you. That's why I'm building The Resilience Protocol Community—a place where entrepreneurs support each other through recovery. Learn more at www.thecomebackguide.com.

Chapter 3: Develop a Resilient Mindset

The Starting Point

That evening when I finally broke down on my couch—the one I described at the start of this book—marked my emotional rock bottom. But it also became the foundation for building something new: a resilient mindset.

During that breakdown, tears streamed down my face. I couldn't stop them. All the pressure, all the pretending, all the fear crashed over me at once. For what felt like hours, I sat there, the reality of my situation finally hitting me with full force.

What terrified me most wasn't the business failing. It was what this failure said about me. Had I wasted years of my life? Was I a fraud? Would everyone see me as incompetent?

These thoughts paralyzed me. I wasn't losing a business, I was losing my identity, my confidence, and my sense of self-worth.

The journey from that breaking point to where I am now wasn't quick or easy. It required completely changing how I thought about failure, success, and my own self-worth. The resilience I developed helped me survive my business closing and prepared me for every challenge that came after.

Why Resilience Matters More Than Success

Resilience isn't helpful for recovery, it's essential. Without it, failure can break you instead of teaching you.

Most of us believe success comes from talent, hard work, or good ideas. These matter, but resilience matters more. Many talented people fail and never try again. Many hardworking people burn out when things get tough. Many brilliant ideas die because their creators couldn't push through setbacks.

Resilience is the ability to:

- Face reality without being crushed by it.
- Learn from setbacks instead of being defined by them.
- Keep moving forward when every instinct says to quit.
- Maintain hope without denying hard truths.
- Rebuild after everything falls apart.

During my breakdown on the couch, I had hit the limit of my resilience. I couldn't bounce back anymore. Each new problem felt like proof I was a failure. Each setback confirmed my worst fears about myself.

This mindset trapped me in a cycle of despair:

- Problem occurs: "This proves I'm a failure."
- Feel overwhelmed: "I can't handle this."
- Avoid reality: "Maybe it will fix itself."
- Things get worse: "See? I'm even more of a failure."

Breaking this cycle required more than positive thinking. It demanded a complete rebuilding of my mental foundation.

Quiz: Your Resilience Scorecard

Rate yourself on these statements from 1 (not at all) to 5 (completely):

1. ___**I can separate who I am from what happened to me.**
   This measures your ability to maintain identity beyond failure. When my business failed, I scored a 1; I felt like I was the failure.
2. ___**I view setbacks as temporary, not permanent.**
   This gauges your perspective on challenges. I scored a 2; each problem felt like a permanent condition.
3. ___**I can find meaning and lessons in difficult experiences.**
   This evaluates your ability to extract value from hardship. I scored a 3; I could see some lessons, but felt they weren't worth the pain.
4. ___**I bounce back quickly after disappointments.**
   This measures your recovery speed. I scored a 1; each setback knocked me down for days or weeks.
5. ___**I believe my actions influence outcomes more than external factors.**
   This assesses your sense of control. I scored a 2; I felt like I was at the mercy of circumstances and didn't have control.

Calculate your score:_____

What your score means:

- **5 – 10:** Your resilience needs significant strengthening. This chapter will help you start.
- **11 – 15:** You have some resilience, but you need to build more robust mental habits.
- **16 – 20:** You have good baseline resilience, but you can strengthen specific areas.
- **21 – 25:** You already have strong resilience. Use this chapter to refine your mental approach.

My first score was 9. After developing a resilient mindset, I scored 18. I still face difficult days, but they no longer define me or my future.

Four Pillars of Mental Resilience

Resilience isn't a trait you're born with—it's built through specific practices. The four pillars I'm about to share create a foundation for bouncing back from any setback.

Many people think resilience means never falling down. That's wrong. Resilience is about how you get back up and what you learned while you were at the bottom.

When my business failed, I didn't have these pillars in place. I had to build them during my darkest moments. You don't have to wait for a crisis to start building yours.

Let's examine each pillar and how to strengthen it.

1. Identity Separation

The first resilience pillar involves separating who you are from what happens to you. This distinction is crucial, yet it's often overlooked.

When my business closed, I lost more than a company—I lost my identity. For years, I'd been "the owner of a cool 3D printing company." When it failed, I felt like I had failed as a person.

This identity fusion creates dangerous vulnerability. When your business and self-worth become the same thing, business problems feel like personal crises.

The healthier approach? Your business can fail without you being a failure. Your career can struggle without you being inadequate.

This separation doesn't happen automatically. It requires conscious effort to build a self-concept based on who you are, not what you do.

Ask yourself:

- Who am I beyond my job title?
- What personal qualities do I value in myself?
- What would still be true about me if my business or career disappeared tomorrow?

- What aspects of myself remain constant despite external changes?

When I first asked these questions, I struggled to answer them. My identity had been so wrapped up in my business that I didn't know who I was without it.

Gradually, I rebuilt my self-concept around enduring qualities:

- I am someone who cares deeply about others.
- I am someone who values learning and growth.
- I am someone who persists despite challenges.
- I am someone who creates and builds things.

These statements remained true whether my business succeeded or failed. They gave me stable ground to stand on while everything else shifted.

Identity Separation Exercise

Create two lists:

1. **What I Do:** roles, titles, achievements
2. **Who I Am:** character traits, values, relationship roles

My lists looked like this:
What I Do:

- Business owner / Entrepreneur
- Production Manager
- Software trainer
- Technical writer
- 3D Designer
- Graphic Designer
- 3D printing specialist
- AI Generalist

Who I Am:

- Caring partner
- Loyal friend

- Creative problem-solver
- Continuous learner
- Person of integrity
- Thoughtful leader
- Resilient survivor

The second list sustains you when the first list changes. When "business owner" disappeared from my first list, I still had everything on my second list.

Discover your Identity

1. Create your "What I Do" and "Who I Am" lists.
2. Identify which items on the "Who I Am" list would remain true even if everything on your "What I Do" list changed.
3. Practice introducing yourself to others using items from your "Who I Am" list, rather than your "What I Do" list.

2. Explanatory Style

The second pillar focuses on how you explain events to yourself. This internal narrative shapes your resilience more than the events themselves.

Psychologists call this your "explanatory style," the way you habitually explain why things happen. Your explanatory style determines whether setbacks crush or strengthen you.

When the company faced problems, my explanatory style made everything worse:

- I saw problems as permanent: "This will never get better."
- I viewed setbacks as pervasive: "Everything is falling apart."
- I took failures personally: "This proves I'm not cut out for business."

This pessimistic explanatory style drained my energy and hope. Each new challenge confirmed my negative beliefs, creating a downward spiral.

A resilient explanatory style looks different:

- You see problems as temporary: "This is difficult now, but I know it won't last forever."

- You view setbacks as specific: "This area is challenging, but I can identify the other things that are working."

- You recognize external factors: "Market conditions played a role in this outcome."

This shift doesn't mean denying reality or avoiding responsibility. It means seeing situations accurately, rather than through the distorting lens of pessimism.

My shift began when a mentor challenged my thinking. After hearing me complain one more time about a lost client, he asked, "Is this really permanent? Is everything truly affected? Are you the only factor in this situation?"

These questions helped me see how my explanatory style was making a difficult situation infinitely worse.

One afternoon, I was on the phone with my business mentor, complaining about losing a client. I remember saying something like, "My business is falling apart. I'm not cut out for sales." He didn't offer sympathy. He stopped me and asked, "Is it all falling apart? Or did you lose one client? Is your whole house on fire, or is there a fire in the kitchen that you need to put out?" That simple reframe; from 'everything' to 'one thing' was a lifeline. It didn't solve the problem, but it made the problem solvable.

Common Thinking Traps

Watch for these thought patterns that undermine resilience:

- **All-or-nothing thinking:** "If we don't get one more client, the business is a failure."
- **Overgeneralization:** "I always make these mistakes. I'll never get it right."
- **Mental filtering:** Focusing only on negatives while ignoring positives
- **Jumping to conclusions:** Assuming the worst without evidence
- **Catastrophizing:** "This small problem will destroy everything."
- **Magical Thinking:** "This next client will save the company."
- **Emotional reasoning:** "I feel like a failure, so I must be one."
- **Should, would, could statements:** "I should have known better." "I would be further along if..." "I could have done something differently."

I caught myself in all these traps. The most damaging trap for me was magical thinking, imagining the next big thing would save the company. When a client made an order, I imagined they would continue ordering and order even more, and more clients would be right behind.

Learning to recognize and challenge these patterns became essential to my resilience.

Thought-Reframing Practice

When negative thoughts arise, use this three-step process:

1. **Identify the thought:**
   "We lost another client. This proves I'm a terrible business owner."
2. **Question its accuracy:**
   "Is this one client truly proof of my overall ability?"
   "Are there factors beyond my control involved?"
   "Have I retained other clients successfully?"
3. **Create a balanced alternative:**
   "Losing this client is disappointing and worth learning from."
   "Some factors were in my control, but others were not."
   "I still have clients who value my work, and I can apply what I've learned going forward."

This practice feels awkward at first. Your brain resists changing established thought patterns. With consistent practice however, a more balanced explanatory style becomes your default.

Reframe your Thinking

1. Identify three negative thoughts you've had about your setback.
2. Apply the three-step reframing process to each thought.
3. Practice catching yourself when you fall into thinking traps.

3. Emotional Regulation

The third pillar involves managing intense emotions without being overwhelmed by them. This skill becomes crucial during failure when feelings run high.

When my business was failing, my emotions controlled me. Anxiety kept me awake at night. Shame made me avoid friends. Fear paralyzed my decision making. These emotional reactions were natural, but my inability to manage them made everything worse.

Emotional regulation doesn't mean suppressing feelings or pretending to be fine. It means experiencing emotions without letting them dictate your actions or consume your thinking.

I learned this skill through necessity. After my breakdown, I realized my emotional state was making rational decisions extremely difficult. I couldn't think clearly enough to plan effectively for what came next.

The breakthrough came when I stopped fighting my emotions and instead learned to work with them.

Emotional-Regulation Strategies

These practices helped me manage overwhelming feelings:

- **Name to tame:** Labeling emotions specifically reduces their intensity. Instead of feeling "bad," I identified feeling "disappointed," "embarrassed," or "uncertain."

- **Physical regulation:** Deep breathing, walking, and simple body movements interrupt the stress cycle. During intense anxiety, I practiced taking a pause, then 10 slow breaths before making decisions.

- **Scheduled worry time:** I set aside 30 minutes daily to worry actively about the business. Outside that time, I postponed worries: "I'll think about that during worry time."

This sounds strange, but it was a game-changer for me. I would set a timer on my phone for 4:00 PM. For those 30 minutes, I gave myself permission to pace around my office and worry about anything and everything. I'd sit with a notepad, or at my computer, and write down what was going through my head. When that timer went off, that was it, stop worrying and continue forward. The rule: You can worry about everything again tomorrow at 4, didn't stop worrying, but it contained it. It stopped it from hijacking my entire day.

- **Emotion diary:** Tracking emotions revealed patterns. I noticed anxiety peaked before the workweek, at the end of a stressful day, and when I checked bank balances.
- **The 10-10-10 rule:** For any decision, I asked, "How will I feel about this in 10 minutes? 10 months? 10 years?" This perspective helped me to see beyond immediate emotions.

These strategies didn't eliminate painful feelings, but they created a pause, a space between emotion and action. This space allowed me to think more clearly and make better decisions.

The Emotional-Wave Technique

When strong emotions hit, try this approach:

- **Acknowledge:** "I'm feeling intense anxiety right now."
- **Accept:** "This feeling is natural, given what I'm facing."
- **Allow:** Let the emotion be present without fighting it.
- **Observe:** Notice physical sensations without judgment.
- **Wait:** Emotions peak and recede like waves if you don't feed them.

I used this technique during panic attacks about business debt. Instead of spiraling into catastrophic thinking, I'd acknowledge the fear, observe my racing heart, and wait for the intensity to naturally decrease.

With practice, emotional waves that once felt overwhelming became manageable. I still felt the full range of emotions, but they no longer control me.

Regulate your Emotional Response

1. Identify your three most frequent difficult emotions.
2. Select one emotional-regulation strategy to practice this week.
3. Use the emotional-wave technique next time you feel overwhelmed.

4. Growth Perspective

The fourth pillar involves viewing challenges as opportunities for growth, rather than proof of inadequacy. This mindset transforms how you experience failure.

When my company began to fail, I saw it purely as a disaster, and proof that I had made terrible choices and wasted years of my life. This perspective made me defensive, closed to feedback, and resistant to change.

The turning point came during a conversation with a mentor who had experienced business failure earlier in his career. "The question isn't whether you failed," he said. "The question is what you'll do with that failure."

This statement helped me to see my situation differently, not as an end but as a beginning with the potential to change my life. Not as a judgment of me, but as feedback for learning. Not as wasted time, but as preparation for what's next.

This growth perspective doesn't minimize the real pain of failure. It acknowledges the pain while also recognizing the potential it brings with it. Here, you ask: "What can I learn from this experience that I couldn't have learned any other way?"

Elements of a Growth Perspective

Adopting a growth perspective involves several mental shifts:

- **From fixed to flexible:** Viewing abilities as changeable through work and learning, not fixed or permanent.
- **From perfection to progress:** Valuing incremental improvement over perfect performance.
- **From avoiding to embracing challenges:** Seeing difficult situations as opportunities.
- **From defending to learning:** Being open to feedback, even when it's painful.
- **From comparison to personal standard:** Measuring yourself against your previous self, not others.

These shifts didn't happen overnight. They emerged gradually as I practiced new ways of thinking about my experiences.

The most difficult shift for me was from defending to learning. My instinct during the business failure—or any failure for that matter—was to justify my decisions and blame external factors. This defensiveness protected my ego but prevented growth. Learning to say, "I made mistakes I can learn from" opened the door to real healing.

Failure-Reframing Questions

These questions helped me extract value from my business failure:

- What skills have I learned through this experience?
- What do I understand now that I didn't before?
- How has this experience helped me to recognize my strengths?
- What would I not have discovered without this challenge?
- How can this prepare me for future opportunities?

Answering these questions revealed unexpected gifts within my failure. I developed skills for handling a crisis, gained insight into financial management, and discovered a resilience I didn't know I had. I also discovered a profound connection with others who were also experiencing setbacks.

These realizations didn't erase the pain of losing my business, but they ensured that the experience wasn't wasted. They transformed a devastating loss into an investment in my future self.

Building on your Strengths

1. Answer the failure-reframing questions about your setback.
2. Identify three specific strengths you've developed through your challenge.
3. Write about how these strengths might serve you in the future.

Building Daily Resilience Habits

Resilience isn't built in moments of crisis. It's built through daily practices that strengthen your mental and emotional foundation before challenges hit.

The four pillars covered require regular maintenance. Like physical fitness, mental resilience develops through consistent habits, not one-time efforts.

After my breakdown, I realized I needed to rebuild my mental resilience from the ground up. Through trial and error, I discovered practices that strengthened my resilience day by day.

These practices won't eliminate problems from your life. They won't prevent all pain or disappointment. What they will do is give you the mental tools to face whatever comes without being broken by it.

Seven Daily Resilience Practices

1. **Morning mental framing:** How you start your day shapes what follows. Begin each morning by naming three things you could control that day, regardless of external circumstances.
2. **Purposeful discomfort:** Small voluntary challenges build tolerance for discomfort. Cold showers, difficult conversations, or learning challenging skills all expand your comfort zone.
3. **Success-failure journaling:** Each evening, write down one success and one setback from the day, along with what you learned from each. This practice helped me extract value from the day's experiences.
4. **Gratitude anchor:** Force yourself to identify three things for which you were genuinely grateful. During my worst business days, this habit prevented negative thinking from taking over.
5. **Physical movement:** The mind-body connection is powerful. Regular exercise, even a 10-minute walk,

reduces stress and improves mental clarity during a crisis.
6. **Progress tracking:** Keeping track of small steps forward maintains momentum. During a crisis, documenting each completed step, no matter how small, is key to resilience and growth.
7. **Connection ritual:** Isolation weakens resilience, but finding people who truly understand business failure can be challenging. Friends and family mean well, but they often don't get what you're experiencing. The Resilience Protocol Community gives you weekly touchpoints with entrepreneurs who've been through this.

Discover more about how you can become part of a growing community at **www.thecomebackguide.com** and experience what it feels like when someone says, 'I know exactly what you mean.

The practice that helped me most was success-failure journaling. It forced me to see that even on my worst days, there was something that went right. And even on my best days, there were lessons to learn. This balanced perspective prevented the one-sided thinking that had previously kept me stuck.

Resilience in Action

Resilience shows up in specific behaviors when facing challenges:

- **Seeking help when needed:** I finally contacted a bankruptcy attorney instead of trying to solve everything alone.

- **Acting despite uncertainty:** I made the decision to close the business even though I didn't have every detail figured out.

- **Focusing energy where it matters:** I stopped trying to save a doomed business and concentrated on what could be learned.
- **Practicing self-compassion:** I learned to speak to myself with the same kindness I would offer a friend in similar circumstances.
- **Finding meaning in difficulty:** I began asking what this experience could teach me, rather than wishing it would end.

These behaviors didn't come naturally at first. They developed through practice and a commitment to building my resilience muscle.

Resilience During Extreme Stress

During the most stressful phases of closing my business, I developed this emergency resilience protocol:

- **Pause:** Stop for 90 seconds and take deep breaths before responding.
- **Check:** Identify what emotional reaction is happening.
- **Ground:** Name five things I can see in my physical environment.
- **Assess:** Ask, "What is truly at stake here?" and, "What can I control?"
- **Act:** Take one small step based on what I can control.

When I received a letter demanding immediate payment of a business loan, this protocol helped me move from panic to productive action. Instead of spiraling into catastrophic thinking, I acknowledged my fear, grounded myself, assessed my options, and called the attorney to find out what needed to be done.

This simple process has helped me handle countless stressful situations since then.

Develop your Resilience Practices

1. Select two daily resilience practices to implement this week.
2. Practice the emergency resilience protocol next time you feel overwhelmed.
3. Identify one relationship that strengthens your resilience and schedule time to nurture it.

Real Results

After developing these resilience practices, I noticed concrete changes in how I handled challenges.

When I talked with friends and my new work colleagues about closing the business and bankruptcy, instead of feeling shame, I explained what happened and what I learned. My response surprised them. They were glad I had been able to turn a negative situation into a learning experience and wanted to learn more about how I did it.

Similarly, when I face health and financial challenges, the same mental tools help me navigate the difficulty without the anxiety that would have previously overwhelmed me. The resilience I built through business failure continues to serve me in completely different contexts.

The most significant change was in my relationship with failure itself. I no longer see failure as something to be feared and avoided at all costs. I see it as valuable feedback, often painful, but always instructive. This perspective has freed me to move in new directions that scared me before.

Creating Your Resilience Plan

Now it's time to create your personal resilience plan by combining elements that resonate with you.

Step 1: Assess your current resilience gaps

Review your score on the Resilience Gap quiz at the beginning of this chapter. Which areas scored lowest? These represent your highest-priority areas for development.

Step 2: Select practices for each pillar

Choose at least one practice from each resilience pillar:

- Identity separation
- Explanatory style
- Emotional regulation
- Growth perspective

Step 3: Establish daily and weekly habits

Decide which practices you'll implement:

- Daily (e.g., morning mental framing)
- Weekly (e.g., success-failure review)
- As needed (e.g., thought reframing)

Step 4: Create emergency protocols

Develop a simple step-by-step process for handling moments of extreme stress or setback.

Step 5: Identify progress measures

How will you know that your resilience is improving?

Examples include:

- Faster recovery from disappointments
- More balanced thinking during setbacks
- Improved ability to separate identity from events

Real Results: The Resilient Mind

Applying these resilience principles transformed my life in remarkable ways. Where I once spiraled for days or weeks after a setback, I now bounce back within hours or at most a day. The nagging questions that used to consume my mental energy; the endless "what-ifs" and rehashing of problems, don't stick around like they used to. My mind has learned to process challenges and move forward rather than getting trapped in unproductive loops. This shift alone has freed up enormous mental bandwidth for constructive thinking and planning.

I completely changed my approach to decision-making. I no longer rely on gut feelings when assessing risks; instead, I objectively identify and evaluate them based on facts and data. When stress hits, I have practical tools that work, like the 90-second break and deep breathing techniques, rather than enduring the overwhelm. I now handle difficult conversations with significantly more ease. Conversations that once filled me with dread no longer do, because I've learned to approach them knowing the outcome will ultimately be beneficial. Most importantly, uncertainty no longer paralyzes me. I face unclear situations with increased confidence because I'm equipped to make sound decisions based on evidence rather than emotion or fear.

Chapter Summary

You built the second essential element of your recovery: a resilient mindset. You've learned that resilience isn't an innate trait, but a set of skills and perspectives that you can develop through practice.

The four pillars; identity separation, explanatory style, emotional regulation, and growth perspective, create a framework for responding to setbacks in ways that lead to growth, rather than defeat. By implementing specific practices within each pillar, you can strengthen your ability to bounce back from any challenge.

Remember that building resilience is an ongoing process, not a one-time exercise. The daily habits and practices discussed gradually reshape how you respond to difficulty. This isn't about pretending failure doesn't hurt; it's about developing the mental tools to move through pain toward growth.

The resilience you build now will not only help you recover from your current setback; it becomes a foundation that supports you through every future challenge. When the next crisis hits, and it will, you'll face it with mental resources you didn't have before.

This Week's Action Steps

1. Complete the Resilience Gap quiz to identify your starting point.
2. Practice identity separation by creating your "What I Do" vs. "Who I Am" lists.
3. Use thought reframing on three negative thoughts about your situation.
4. Implement one emotional-regulation strategy when you feel overwhelmed.
5. Answer the failure-reframing questions to find growth opportunities.

Key Takeaways

- Resilience comes from specific skills and practices, not personality traits.

- Separating who you are from what happens to you creates stability during change.

- How you explain events to yourself shapes your ability to recover from them.

- Managing emotions without being controlled by them enables clearer thinking.

- Viewing setbacks as opportunities for growth transforms how you experience failure.

Reflection Question

Which resilience pillar will make the biggest difference in your recovery if you strengthen it this week?

The next chapter builds on your resilient mindset by showing you how to set clear, achievable goals that move you from recovery to your next venture.

With your resilient mindset developing, you're ready to set goals that actually work. Now that your mindset is fortified, it's time to aim your energy. The next chapter is about building a roadmap out of the wilderness.

A Note About Community"

The exercises in this chapter work. I used them myself. But they work better when you're surrounded by people doing them with you. That's why I'm building The Resilience Protocol Community—a place where entrepreneurs support each other through recovery. Learn more at www.thecomebackguide.com.

Chapter 4: Set Clear, Achievable Goals

Lost Without Direction

I felt lost. The daily routine of running a business, checking emails, talking to clients, and managing projects ended. I'd wake up each morning with no clear purpose. The question, "What now?" played constantly in my head.

About three weeks after the business closed, I was at my desk, intent on formulating my next plan. But from my computer screen, a blank Word document glowered back at me. I was trying, but my mind kept jumping between scattered ideas.

"Maybe I should start another business." "I could look for a job in 3D printing." "Perhaps I should change my career completely." "What should I focus on?"

None of these ideas stuck. I'd write down an idea, then immediately doubt it. By the end of a few hours, I had a document full of cool ideas, but no plan for any of them. I didn't want to repeat the past where each idea was started, then abandoned for the next idea.

The pressure to "figure it all out" felt overwhelming. In my head, I thought society expects quick rebounds from failure. Friends and family meant well with questions like, "What's next?" and, "Do you have a plan yet?" But each question only emphasized how lost I felt.

Thankfully, I landed a training development contract that provided me with a stable income for at least a few months. So, for a while, my days weren't completely without structure or direction. However, after the initial contract ended, my days became unproductive. I'd spend time researching business ideas, looking at job listings, or distracting myself with TV and social media. This aimlessness only deepened my sense of failure.

What I didn't realize when I opened the Word document was that I was making a common mistake, trying to imagine an entire new life path in one sitting. The scale of that task guaranteed confusion and frustration. What I needed wasn't a perfect plan, but rather a set of clear, achievable goals that would move me forward one step at a time.

My breakthrough came during a conversation with a friend who ran a design company. "You wouldn't build a house without plans," he said. "And you wouldn't try to build it in an afternoon. So, why are you doing that for your next step?"

That question shifted my perspective. I didn't need all the answers at once. I needed a structured approach to setting my goals, a way to convert the noise in my head into concrete, manageable steps.

The Goal-Setting Problem After Failure

Setting goals after a major failure presents unique challenges that often are overlooked in typical goal-setting advice.

Many goal-setting guides assume you're starting from a position of stability and strength. They don't account for the emotional and practical obstacles you face after failure:

- **Confidence deficit:** After failure, self-doubt makes setting ambitious goals feel futile. "Why bother trying again?" becomes a persistent thought.

- **Fear of commitment:** Setting new goals means risking failure again. This fear can paralyze your decision making.

- **Urgency vs. clarity:** Financial pressures create urgency that clouds judgment. You panic and feel that you must act quickly, even without clarity.
- **Identity confusion:** Without your previous role, you may not know what goals align with who you are without your business.
- **Limited resources:** Failure often depletes financial and emotional reserves, restricting your options.
- **External expectations:** Others expect you to "bounce back" quickly with your life and future, adding pressure.

Facing all of these obstacles, my confidence was shattered. Each potential goal came with the fear: "What if I fail at this too?" The financial pressure wasn't immediate, but I would need a source of income within a few months. I had to remember that rushing into decisions had gotten me into trouble before.

The most challenging aspect was the identity question. For years, my goals had been centered around growing the company. Without that anchor, I wasn't sure what I would be aiming for.

Common Goal-Setting Mistakes After Failure

In this vulnerable state, it's easy to fall into counterproductive goal-setting patterns:

1. **Setting vague goals:** "Find success again" and, "Get back on my feet" lack the specificity needed for action.

2. **Setting unrealistic goals:** Trying to recover financial losses immediately with an ambitious new venture.

3. **Setting purely reactive goals:** Choosing paths based solely on avoiding past mistakes, rather than moving toward something meaningful.

4. **Setting goals based on others' expectations:** Pursuing goals to impress others instead of what truly matters to you.

5. **Setting too many goals at once:** Overwhelming yourself with a complete life overhaul instead of focused progress.

6. **Setting goals without accounting for reality:** Ignoring financial constraints, market conditions, and personal limitations.

I made several of these mistakes in my first attempts at post-failure planning. First, I set a vague goal of "rebuilding my life" without specifics. I considered launching an ambitious business venture even before I examined the problems with the first one. I created an impossible list of non-specific goals: find income, get in shape, start a new business, and rebuild my life, all within unrealistic timeframes.

Quiz: Goal Setting Gap

Rate yourself on these statements from 1 (not at all) to 5 (completely):

1. ___**I have specific, written goals for my recovery.**
   Do you have clear targets, or general hopes or desires?

2. ___**My goals include measurable elements.**

   Can you track your progress with numbers, dates, or other concrete metrics?

3. ___**My goals feel challenging but achievable.**

   Are they realistic, given your current situation?

4. ___**My goals align with my personal values.**

   Do they reflect what matters most to you, not external measures of success?

5. ___**I've broken down my goals into specific action steps.**

   Do you know exactly what to do next?

Calculate your score:_____

What your score means:

- **5 – 10:** You need a complete goal setting reset.
- **11 – 15:** You have some direction but need more structure.
- **16 – 20:** You have a good foundation on which build.
- **21 – 25:** Your goal setting approach is strong.

My first score after trying to plan my future? A low 7. I had ideas, but no real structure or clarity. After implementing the approach that I'll share with you, my score increased to 19! And with continued refinement and effort, it will be even higher.

The SMART+ Goal Framework

The path forward begins with a structured approach to goal setting that addresses the unique challenges of post-failure recovery.

You've likely heard of SMART goals before: Specific, Measurable, Achievable, Relevant, and Time-bound. This framework provides a solid foundation; however, after failure, we need to expand it further.

Let me introduce a variation—the SMART+ framework, which adds two crucial elements needed for post-failure recovery:

- **Specific:** Clearly defined objective
- **Measurable:** Concrete way to track progress
- **Achievable:** Realistic given your current situation
- **Relevant:** Aligned with your values and larger aims
- **Time-bound:** Has a defined timeline
- **+Values:** Connected to your core values
- **+Adaptable:** Flexible enough to adjust as circumstances change

Let's explore how to apply each element to your recovery goals:

1. Specific Goals Provide Clarity

Vague aspirations such as, "find success again" don't tell you what to do next. Specific goals give you clarity about exactly what you're working toward.

Ask yourself:

- What precisely do I want to accomplish?
- What actions will this goal require?
- Who might be involved in this goal?
- Where will this goal take place?
- Which resources or limitations are involved?

When I first tried planning after the company closed, my goal was simply "rebuild my life." This gave me no direction.

I revised one of my goals to "Develop the content for a book based on my experience from closing my business and recovering from the failure within 4 months." This specific goal gave me immediate clarity about what actions to take.

Make your goals specific by completing this sentence: "I will [action verb] [detailed outcome] by [specific timeframe]."

2. Measurable Progress Builds Momentum

Measurable goals allow you to track progress, which builds confidence through visible movement forward.

Ask yourself:

- How will I know when this goal is achieved?
- What metrics can I use to track progress?
- How can I break this down into measurable milestones?

My vague goal of "rebuilding my life" had no measurable elements. I couldn't tell if I was making progress.

I revised this to include "establish an outline within 1 week," "write the content for the first chapter within 3 weeks," and "complete all chapter first drafts within 2 months." These metrics gave me clear ways to measure progress even before reaching the final goal.

For each goal, identify at least two metrics you'll use to track progress.

3. Achievable Goals Rebuild Confidence

After failure, it's crucial to set goals that stretch you while remaining achievable. Early wins rebuild the confidence needed for bigger challenges.

Ask yourself:

- Is this goal realistic, given my current situation?
- Do I have or can I access the necessary resources?
- What obstacles might prevent achievement, and how can I address them?
- Have I set the bar at the correct height?

One of my post-failure mistakes was setting one goal as, "Start a new business that replaces my previous income within six months." This wasn't realistic, given my emotional situation and the bankruptcy process.

I revised this to, "Research viable business models while securing steady income from contract work." This achievable approach meant I could explore entrepreneurship without financial pressure.

Be honest about your current resources, skills, and circumstances when setting goals. It's better to achieve modest goals than to fail at ambitious ones, especially during recovery.

My first attempt at a goal, written in a panic-fueled daze, was: 'Launch a new business that replaces my previous income in six months.' It was a fantasy. My confidence was so shattered that the size of this goal paralyzed me from doing anything productive. So, I threw it out. My first real, achievable goal? 'Take a walk around the neighborhood today.' That's it. I did it. That tiny, achievable win, that feeling of 'I said I would do a thing, and I did it,' was the first brick I laid in my new foundation. We don't rebuild our lives with giant leaps; we do it with one small, steady step after another.

4. Relevant Goals Connect to Your Journey

Every goal should move you forward on your recovery journey and align with your broader life direction.

Ask yourself:

- Does this goal matter in my overall life context?
- Will this goal move me toward where I want to be?
- Is this the right time for this particular goal?

- Does this goal support my other goals?

Briefly, I considered the goal of pursuing a bachelor's degree in entrepreneurship (I already have an associate's degree in entrepreneurship). While potentially valuable, this wasn't relevant to my immediate needs of financial stability and rebuilding my confidence.

Instead, I focused on goals directly related to rebuilding my personal identity, income, and relationships, all of which were immediately relevant to my recovery journey.

For each goal you set, explain to yourself why it matters to your overall recovery and long-term direction.

5. Time-bound Goals Create Urgency

Goals without deadlines tend to drift. Time boundaries create productive urgency and prevent procrastination.

Ask yourself:

- By when do I want to achieve this goal?
- What's a realistic timeframe, given my circumstances?
- Which intermediate deadlines can I set for milestones?
- Is this timeline motivating without being stressful?

My initial vague desire to "write a book about my experience" without a timeline created neither structure nor urgency.

When I revised this to specific timeframes—"establish an outline within 1 week," "write the content for the first chapter within 3 weeks," and "complete all chapter first drafts within 2 months"—I gave myself specific deadlines. These deadlines allowed me to create milestones and track my progress.

Set specific deadlines for both your overall goals and the milestones along the way.

6. Values-Aligned Goals Provide Meaning

The "+" in SMART+ begins with values alignment. Goals that connect to your core values provide motivation beyond any external rewards.

Ask yourself:

- Which values are most important to me?
- Does this goal stay true to those values?
- Will achieving this goal bring meaningful satisfaction?
- Am I pursuing this for myself or to impress others?

After my self-assessment, the core values I identified were rich relationships, creativity, financial security, continuous learning, and work–life balance.

I made sure my goals aligned with these values. Rather than aiming for the highest-paying job or seeking out the next "big thing," it's more important to me to find a balance between fair compensation with creative work and reasonable hours.

For each goal, identify which personal values it supports and how achieving it will bring meaning beyond external success.

7. Adaptable Goals Respond to Reality

The second "+" element is adaptability. Recovery rarely follows a straight line, so your goals need built-in flexibility.

Ask yourself:

- How might this goal be affected if circumstances change?
- Which alternative approaches could I take, if needed?
- Which indicators would tell me that a goal needs adjustment?
- Am I prepared to modify this goal without seeing it as failure?

Because I had some contract work, my initial goals were based more on health, wellness, and longer-term planning. However, as income became a higher priority later in the year, I adapted my goals to include creating content for books and lessons where my skills applied.

Build flexibility into your goals by identifying potential pivot points and alternative paths toward your larger objectives.

The Goal Hierarchy: From Vision to Daily Tasks

Goals don't exist in isolation. They form part of a connected hierarchy from the big picture to daily tasks.

Many people make the mistake of setting disconnected goals that don't build toward anything larger. Or, conversely, they set only big visions without actionable steps.

The goal hierarchy connects your daily actions to your larger purpose, providing both meaning and practical direction. It consists of four levels.

1. Vision Statement: Your North Star

A vision statement describes the future you're working toward. It's not necessarily achievable in the short term, but it guides all other goals.

After much reflection following the company's closure, my vision became, "Build a flexible career that provides financial security while allowing me to use my creative and technical skills to help others, maintaining balance between work accomplishment and personal fulfillment."

This vision wasn't immediately achievable, but it gave direction to all of my other goals. It incorporated my values of creativity, financial stability, service, and work–life balance.

Your vision statement should feel personally meaningful and emotionally resonant. It should answer the question, "What kind of life am I trying to create?"

To craft your vision statement, complete this sentence: "I am working toward a life in which I [describe the future you want to create]."

2. Long–term Goals: Your 1 – 3 Year Horizons

Long-term goals break your vision into major milestones that are achievable within 1 – 3 years. They bridge the gap between your ideal future and the present.

My long-term goals included:

- Establish a stable income stream through employment or a business.
- Build my professional reputation in a field to which I feel connected.
- Develop new skills in an area that expands my career options.
- Rebuild my savings so I can have a secure retirement.

Each of these goals directly supported my overall vision while breaking it down into achievable chunks. They gave me a sense of direction without overwhelming me.

Your long-term goals should represent significant progress toward your vision while remaining realistic, given your current situation.

For each aspect of your vision, identify one long-term goal that would represent meaningful progress in that area.

3. Short–term Goals: Your 30 – 90 Day Focus

Short-term goals translate your long-term objectives into immediate focus areas. These are your priorities for the next 30 – 90 days.

For my long-term goal of establishing stable income, my short-term goals were:

- Update my website to promote my new company, AI Performance Partners, within 15 days.

- Attend 5 networking events and connect with at least 10 new people within 30 days.
- Complete the first draft of this book within 45 days.
- Secure 3 new clients within 60 days.
- Begin new contract work within 90 days.

These short-term goals created a clear roadmap for my immediate future. Each morning, I knew exactly what I should be working on.

Your short-term goals should follow the complete SMART+ framework and directly support your long-term objectives.

For each long-term goal, identify 1 – 3 short-term goals that would move you substantially closer to achievement.

4. Weekly and Daily Tasks: Your Immediate Actions

Tasks break your short-term goals into specific actions that you'll take this week, tomorrow, or today. They answer the question, "What exactly should I do now?"

For my short-term goal of updating my website, my weekly tasks included:

- Days 1 – 2: Develop the website map and determine the visual style.
- Days 3 – 4: Gather all previous work samples and organize by category.
- Days 5 – 7: Select 5 best examples that showcase my services.
- Days 8 – 10: Write content for homepage.
- Days 11 – 12: Create the prototype website and upload content.
- Days 13 – 14: Get feedback from 2 – 3 trusted contacts and revise.

These specific tasks eliminated guesswork about what to do each day. They transformed my recovery from an overwhelming challenge into a series of manageable actions.

Your weekly and daily tasks should be concrete, specific actions that can be completed in a single sitting and clearly marked as done.

For each short-term goal, create a list of sequential tasks that will lead to its completion.

Aligning Goals with Your New Reality

After failure, setting effective goals requires honest acknowledgment of your new circumstances. Your goals must align with your current reality, not the reality that you wish existed. This alignment involves several practical considerations.

1. Financial Reality Check

After the company closed, my financial reality changed dramatically. I had bankruptcy proceedings, damaged credit, and little savings. Thankfully, I did have a short-term contract that provided income.

My initial goals ignored these constraints. I considered goals that required immediate investment or lengthy periods without income, both impossible in my situation.

I needed to adjust my goals to my financial reality. This meant prioritizing income through my contract work before pursuing longer-term business development. It also meant choosing options with low costs, rather than those requiring significant investment.

Conduct your own financial reality check by answering:

- What is my current available cash?
- What monthly income do I need to cover essentials?
- Which debts or obligations require immediate attention?

- How long can I sustain myself without new income?
- Which financial restrictions limit my options?

Let your answers shape your goals. If you need immediate income, prioritize goals that generate revenue quickly. If you have financial breathing room, you might prioritize skills development or exploration.

2. Skills and Experience Inventory

Your experience isn't erased by failure. You have transferable skills and knowledge that should be a part of your goal setting.

After the closure, I conducted a detailed inventory of my skills. I identified strengths in training development, 3D design, 3D printing, technical problem-solving, and an understanding of AI. These became the foundation for my career goals, rather than starting from scratch in an unrelated field.

Create your own skills inventory by listing:

- Technical skills you've developed.
- Soft skills you've demonstrated.
- Industry knowledge you've acquired.
- Problems you've successfully solved.
- Connections and relationships you've built.

Use this inventory to set goals that leverage your existing strengths while determining gaps. This approach builds on your foundation, rather than completely starting over.

3. Personal Circumstances Assessment

Your goals must account for personal circumstances beyond financial and professional factors.

My personal circumstances included:

- A supportive spouse who provided emotional stability.
- No children or dependents requiring support.

- Health concerns that need attention after prolonged stress.
- Limited family obligations.
- Ability to travel.

These factors influenced my goals in various ways. The emotional support allowed me to take some down-time and think about what's next. The health concerns meant I needed to include wellness goals alongside career objectives. The ability to travel opened options that wouldn't be available to someone who is stuck at home or has commitments that keep them from traveling.

Assess your own personal circumstances by considering:

- Family obligations and support
- Geographic constraints or opportunities
- Health and wellness needs
- Time availability and constraints
- Emotional support systems

Adjust your goals to work with these realities, rather than against them. Goals that conflict with personal circumstances rarely succeed.

4. Market and Industry Assessment

Finally, your goals must align with external market realities.

I researched current demands in my industry and discovered that, while the exact role I had before was scarce, related positions in training content and AI development were growing. This market reality shaped my career goals toward these adjacent opportunities.

Research your own market realities by investigating:

- Current demand for your skills and experience.
- Growth areas related to your background.
- Entry requirements for fields you're considering.
- Compensation ranges and expectations.
- Geographic distribution of opportunities.

Let market realities inform which goals are most likely to succeed. Even the most well-crafted goal will fail if it doesn't align with external demand.

Goal-Setting Implementation Plan

Now, let's put everything together into a practical implementation plan for setting your recovery goals.

Step 1: Create Your Goal Foundation (1 – 2 days)

Begin by establishing the foundation for all your goals:

- Write your vision statement.
- Complete your financial reality check.
- Create your skills and experience inventory.
- Assess your personal circumstances.
- Research relevant market realities.

This foundational work might seem time-consuming when you're eager to move forward, but it prevents wasted effort on misaligned goals.

Step 2: Develop Your Goal Hierarchy (2 – 3 days)

With your foundation in place, create your goal hierarchy:

- Set 3 – 5 long-term goals (1 – 3 years) that support your vision.
- Develop 2 – 3 short-term goals (30 – 90 days) for each long-term goal.
- Break each short-term goal into weekly and daily tasks.

Make sure each goal follows the SMART+ framework. Check that each level connects logically to the levels above and below it.

Step 3: Create Accountability Systems (1 day)

Goals without accountability often remain unfulfilled. Establish systems to keep yourself on track:

- Select a tracking method (journal, app, spreadsheet).
- Identify accountability partners for different goals.
- Schedule regular review sessions (weekly, monthly).
- Create visible reminders of your goals.
- Determine how you'll measure progress.

I used a simple spreadsheet to track my goals, with monthly review sessions with my accountability partner to keep me on track.

Step 4: Implement Your First Week's Tasks (7 days)

Begin immediate implementation of the tasks supporting your most pressing short-term goals:

- Schedule specific times for each task.
- Create the environment needed for completion.
- Remove obstacles before starting.
- Track completion and results.
- Adjust as needed based on what you learn.

The sooner you move from planning to action, the quicker you'll build momentum.

Step 5: Conduct Your First Weekly Review (1 hour)

After your first week, conduct a structured review:

- Which tasks did you complete?
- Which challenges arose?
- What did you learn that might affect your goals?
- Which adjustments are needed?
- What are your priorities for the coming week?

Use this review to refine your approach going forward.

Real Results: Your Goal-Setting Journey

After implementing this goal-setting framework, your recovery journey will take a more structured and productive direction.

With a foundation established, move on to your next short-term goal. Again, use the SMART+ framework; research options, consult advisors, and create a structured schedule.

Each achieved goal builds momentum for the next. More importantly, the goal-setting process itself helps to restore your sense of control and direction. Even before reaching your targets, having clarity about where you are heading will reduce anxiety and increase daily productivity.

The contrast between my aimless first weeks and my structured approach after implementing this framework was dramatic. In the first case, I spent days in unproductive worry. In the second, each day had clear purpose and moved me measurably forward.

Chapter Summary

This chapter has guided you through creating a structured goal-setting framework that addresses the unique challenges of recovery after failure. You've explored how typical goal-setting approaches often fall short when you're rebuilding from a significant setback, and how the expanded SMART+ framework provides the structure and meaning needed during this critical time.

The goal hierarchy, from broad vision to daily tasks, creates a roadmap that connects your immediate actions to your larger purpose, transforming overwhelming challenges into manageable steps. By aligning your goals with your current reality rather than wishful thinking, you set yourself up for sustainable progress rather than further disappointment.

Remember that effective goal setting after failure isn't about achievement; it's about restoring your sense of direction, purpose, and control. Even before reaching your targets, the clarity that comes from well-structured goals reduces anxiety and increases productive action.

This Week's Action Steps

6. Complete the Goal-Setting Gap Quiz to determine your starting point.
7. Write your vision statement that will guide all other goals.
8. Conduct your financial reality check to understand your constraints.
9. Create one long-term goal (1 – 3 years) that supports your vision.
10. Develop one short-term goal (30 – 90 days) that moves you toward your long-term goal.
11. Break your short-term goal into specific tasks for the next seven days.
12. Implement your first task tomorrow.

Key Takeaways

- The SMART+ framework expands traditional goal setting to include values alignment and adaptability—both crucial after failure.

- Your goal hierarchy connects daily actions to your larger purpose, providing both meaning and practical direction.

- Goals must align with your current reality—financial, personal, and market—not the reality you wish existed.

Reflection Question

Which single goal, if achieved within the next 90 days, would most significantly move your recovery forward?

The next chapter builds on your goal-setting framework to create a comprehensive recovery plan that integrates all aspects of rebuilding your life after failure.

Clear goals need a clear plan. Let's build yours. You have your destination. Now you need the vehicle. The next chapter shows you how to build an actionable plan to get there.

A Note About Community"

The exercises in this chapter work. I used them myself. But they work better when you're surrounded by people doing them with you. That's why I'm building The Resilience Protocol Community—a place where entrepreneurs support each other through recovery. Learn more at www.thecomebackguide.com.

Chapter 5: Create an Actionable Recovery Plan

From Overwhelm to Action

The day after I decided to close the company, I woke up feeling lost. My business had been my daily focus for years. Now what? I sat at my computer with a blank Word document open in front of me. But I was frozen. Too many questions ran through my head.

What would I do for income? How would I handle the debt? What should I tell clients? When should I inform vendors? These questions swirled in my mind, each one triggering new worries.

My wife found me still sitting there an hour later, the page still blank. "What's wrong?" she asked.

"I don't know where to start," I admitted. "There's way too much to think about."

She sat down across from me. "Don't try to figure it all out at once. Think about the first thing you need to do."

That simple advice broke my paralysis. The first thing? Contact my attorney about the closing process. I wrote it down. The second? Talk to my employee. I wrote that down too.

One by one, actions replaced overwhelm. By the end of the day, I had a list of ten specific tasks. It wasn't a complete plan, but it was a start. Each item gave me one clear step to take.

That list became the basis for my recovery plan. It evolved from those initial ten tasks into a structured approach for closing the business, handling the debt, and rebuilding my life. Without it, I might have remained frozen by indecision or acted impulsively out of panic.

A recovery plan won't eliminate the pain of failure, but it gives you direction when you feel lost. It transforms vague fears into specific challenges you can address. Most importantly, it puts you back in control when everything feels chaotic.

Why Most Recovery Attempts Fail

Many people try to bounce back from failure without a clear plan. Their recovery efforts often fail for predictable reasons.

1. Reacting vs. Responding

After failure, our instinct is to react quickly to escape the pain. I almost jumped right back into starting a new business, even though doing so would clearly be a repeat of my past mistakes.

Reacting happens when:

- You make decisions based on short-term relief.
- Fear drives your choices.
- You jump into action without reflection.
- You try to escape feelings, rather than process them.

2. Trying to Fix Everything at Once

When your life falls apart everything is urgent. Without priorities, you spread your energy too thin and accomplish little.

I initially tried to address all my problems simultaneously:

- Find a new income source.
- Process my grief over the business.
- Handle my mounting debt.
- Repair my strained relationships.
- Manage my health issues from stress.

This scattered approach left me exhausted and discouraged. Nothing improved because I couldn't focus enough energy on any single area.

3. Lacking Concrete Next Steps

Vague goals like "find a new job" or "pay off debt" aren't enough. Without specific actions, you stay stuck in the planning phase.

My early attempts at planning included goals like:

- Build a better company
- Recover financially
- Reduce stress

These goals sounded good, but they gave me no clear direction. I couldn't measure progress or know what to do each day.

4. Missing Accountability Structures

Plans without accountability rarely survive contact with reality. When motivation wavers or obstacles appear, it's easy to abandon your plan.

I wrote many "plans" in notebooks that never became action because:

- I didn't set deadlines for specific tasks.
- No one knew what I had committed to.
- I had no regular check-in system.
- I created no consequences for inaction.

5. Ignoring Emotional Recovery

Many recovery plans focus only on practical concerns like finances and career while neglecting emotional healing.

My first plans addressed financial issues but ignored:

- Processing grief over the lost business.
- Rebuilding my confidence.
- Addressing sleep problems and anxiety.
- Repairing strained relationships.

This imbalance undermined my progress. Unaddressed emotions drained the energy I needed for action.

Quiz: Diagnose Your Planning Approach

Rate yourself on these statements from 1 (not at all) to 5 (completely):

1. ___**I have clear, specific next steps, rather than vague goals.**
   This measures whether you know what actions to take tomorrow.

2. ___**My plan balances quick wins with long-term solutions.**
   This reveals whether your plan builds momentum while addressing root causes.

3. ___**I've established concrete ways to track my progress.**
   This shows if you can objectively measure your advancement.

4. ___**My plan includes both practical tasks and emotional recovery.**
   This indicates whether your plan addresses your whole person.

5. ___**I've built in accountability to keep me on track.**
   This measures whether your plan includes support for follow-through.

Calculate your score:_____

What your score means:

- **5 – 10:** Your planning approach needs significant strengthening.
- **11 – 15:** You have some elements of effective planning, but gaps remain.
- **16 – 20:** You have a solid planning foundation, but can refine your approach.
- **21 – 25:** You have an excellent planning system and should focus on execution.

My initial score? Only a 6. I had some vague goals but no specific steps, accountability, or emotional components. After developing a proper recovery plan, I scored 19. There's still room for improvement, but the difference in my progress was dramatic.

The Five Components of an Effective Recovery Plan

An effective recovery plan goes beyond a simple to-do list. It provides structure when your life feels chaotic and direction when you feel lost. Based on what worked for me and others who have successfully rebuilt after failure, there are five essential components to include.

1. Stabilization Priorities

When everything is urgent, you need clear priorities. Stabilization focuses on stopping further damage and securing basic needs before tackling larger goals.

My stabilization priorities included:

- Finding temporary income to cover essential bills.
- Contacting my attorney to get bankruptcy advice.
- Addressing immediate health concerns from stress.
- Building emotional support from key relationships.

Your stabilization phase isn't about solving all your problems. It's about creating enough security to think clearly about long-term recovery.

For each area of your life affected by failure, ask:

- What immediate actions would prevent things from getting worse?
- Which basic needs must be met for me to function effectively?
- Which temporary solutions would buy me time to develop permanent ones?

Resist the urge to skip this step. Without stabilization, you'll remain in crisis mode, making reactive decisions rather than strategic ones.

Before this step, my mind was a whirlwind of equally urgent tasks: call the lawyer, talk to vendors, find income, tell my family, fix my health... I was completely frozen by the sheer volume of it. The 'Stabilization Priorities' exercise was my fire extinguisher. It forced me to ask, 'What is on fire right now? What will cause the most damage if I don't address it in the next 48 hours?'

The answer wasn't everything. It was: 'Secure enough contract work to pay the bills this month.' That became my top priority. Suddenly, the chaos had an anchor point. Everything else could wait.

2. The 30-60-90 Day Framework

Recovery happens in stages, not all at once. Breaking your plan into 30-day increments creates manageable chunks and allows for adjustments based on what's working.

My framework looked like this:

First 30 Days: Emergency Response

- Secure contract work for basic income.
- Complete business closure paperwork.
- Schedule initial consultation with bankruptcy attorney.
- Establish daily stress management routine.
- Inform all relevant stakeholders about the business closure.

Days 31 – 60: Foundation Building

- Take time to allow my body and mind to rest and recover.
- Create a budget based on new financial reality.
- Begin regular meetings with support network.
- Set up a system to track progress and emotional state.
- Complete bankruptcy filing process.

Days 61 – 90: Forward Movement

- Explore career/business options aligned with core strengths.
- Increase income through additional work opportunities.
- Establish a new personal identity separate from the failed business.
- Develop a long-term financial recovery strategy.
- Create a sustainable work-life balance.

This framework doesn't limit you to these timeframes. Some goals may take longer, while others happen faster. The point is, creating clear expectations about what happens when prevents the common "everything must change immediately" mindset that leads to burnout.

3. Balance of Quick Wins and Deep Work

Your recovery plan needs both:

- Quick wins that build confidence and momentum.
- Deep work that addresses root issues.

I struggled with this balance. My first plans focused only on urgent problems, which created a perpetual cycle of crisis management without lasting progress. Later plans swung too far toward long-term goals without the immediate successes needed to sustain motivation.

The right mix includes at least one quick win each week alongside steady progress on deeper issues. A more balanced approach included:

Quick Wins:

- Securing a contract for work within my first week of planning.
- Setting up a simple system to track expenses and regain financial control.
- Creating a morning routine that reduces anxiety.
- Reaching out to one professional contact each week to rebuild my network.

Deep Work:

- Bi-weekly sessions with a counselor to identify sustainable paths forward.
- Regular financial review and planning sessions.
- Developing new skills identified during my self-assessment.

- Building habits to manage stress long-term.

Quick wins provided the energy and confidence for deeper work. Deep work ensured that my recovery created lasting change, instead of temporary relief.

I'll give you a perfect example from one of my toughest weeks. My 'quick win' was simple: cleaning and organizing my disaster of a home office. It took two hours, but having a clean, orderly space gave me a huge mental boost and a tangible sense of control. That energy then fueled my 'deep work' for the week: a two-hour session digging into the final bankruptcy paperwork, which was emotionally draining but absolutely necessary. The quick win literally paid for the deep work. Without that initial boost, I would have kept procrastinating on the harder task.

4. Progress Metrics and Tracking System

What gets measured, gets improved. Clear metrics help you recognize progress when emotional turmoil might otherwise blind you to moving forward.

My initial plan lacked concrete ways to measure progress. I'd worked for weeks feeling like nothing was changing, destroying my motivation. Once I established specific metrics, I could see even small forward progress.

Effective recovery metrics must be:

- Objective, rather than subjective
- Measurable in specific units (money, time, frequency, etc.)
- Within your direct control
- Tracked regularly

My tracking system included:

- Weekly income vs. expenses
- Hours spent on skill development

- Number of new professional connections made
- Sleep quality score (1 – 10 scale)
- Daily stress level (1 – 10 scale)
- Number of action items completed each week

I reviewed these metrics every other Monday, noting patterns and adjusting my plan based on what the data showed. This regular review prevented the common mistake of continuing ineffective approaches simply because they're part of the plan.

5. Accountability Structure

Even the best plan fails without accountability. When motivation inevitably wavers, your accountability structure keeps you moving forward.

My accountability structure had three layers:

Personal Accountability:

- Daily written commitment to my three most important tasks.
- Evening review of completed actions.
- Weekly progress assessment against 30/60/90-day goals.
- Accounting for missed actions.

Partner Accountability:

- Regular check-in with my wife about plan progress.
- Permission for her to ask direct questions about relevant steps.

External Accountability:

- Monthly meeting with a mentor/counselor to review progress.
- Commitments shared with a trusted friend who would check in.

- Public commitments to selected individuals about delivery dates.

The most effective element was my regular check-in with my wife. Since she knew the recovery plan, she could ask specific questions, rather than general ones.

Without accountability, it's too easy to let discomfort derail your plan. The temporary relief of avoidance feels good in that moment, but it prevents long-term recovery.

Creating Your Recovery Plan

Now, let's build your personal recovery plan using the five components.

Step 1: Conduct a Recovery Inventory

Before planning, assess your current situation objectively. This inventory identifies what needs immediate attention and what can wait.

Areas to inventory:

- Financial situation (income, expenses, debt, assets)
- Career status (skills, credentials, network, opportunities)
- Health indicators (physical symptoms, energy, sleep quality)
- Relationship health (support available, strained connections)
- Mental state (stress level, clarity, focus ability)

For each area, note:

- Current status (use specific measures where possible)
- Most pressing issues that require attention
- Available resources you can leverage
- Initial steps already taken

This inventory forms the foundation of your stabilization priorities. It reveals where to focus first, rather than trying to address everything all at once.

Step 2: Set Your Stabilization Priorities

Review your inventory and identify issues that:

- Present immediate threats if they are not addressed.
- Block progress in multiple areas.
- Must be resolved before other recovery work can begin.
- Affect your basic functioning and well-being.

These become your stabilization priorities. For each one, define:

1. **One specific action to take within 48 hours.**

   For example, rather than "deal with debt," specify "call credit card company to request hardship program."

2. **Success criteria for initial stabilization.**

   What specific, measurable condition would indicate this area is stable enough to shift focus elsewhere?

3. **Resources required.**

   What information, assistance, or tools do you need to take action?

4. **Estimated time to reach a stable point.**

   How long before this area reaches your defined stability point?

Keep this list focused. Three to five priorities are sufficient for most situations. Adding more creates the scattered approach we're trying to avoid.

Step 3: Develop Your 30/60/90-Day Framework

Now, map out progressive action over the next 90 days. For each 30-day period, identify:

1. **Three primary focus areas**

    Select areas from your inventory that make sense to address during this period.

2. **Specific goals for each focus area**

    What measurable outcomes will you achieve in this timeframe?

3. **Key actions required**

    What specific steps will lead to these outcomes?

4. **Resources needed**

    What support, information, or tools must you acquire?

For the first 30 days, emphasize your stabilization priorities. Days 31 – 60 should build a foundation for longer-term recovery. Days 61 – 90 should begin shifting toward your next chapter, rather than recovering from the previous one.

Step 4: Balance Quick Wins with Deep Work

Review your 30/60/90-day framework and ensure it includes both:

At least one quick win each week

Identify actions that:

- Can be completed in a single day.

- Produce tangible, visible results.
- Build confidence through success.
- Remove immediate pain points.

Ongoing deep work in key areas

Schedule regular time for activities that:

- Address root causes rather than symptoms.
- Build capabilities for long-term success.
- Prevent similar failures in the future.
- Create sustainable change.

Maintain this balance throughout your plan. When motivation lags or progress slow, quick wins provide much-needed momentum. Deep work ensures that momentum leads to lasting change.

Step 5: Establish Your Tracking System

Create a simple system to measure progress in each focus area. Effective tracking includes:

Weekly metrics review

Schedule a specific time each week to review all your metrics.

Visual progress representation

Create a dashboard, chart, or other visual display showing movement over time. Spreadsheets, mind-mapping, sticky notes, or any preferred kind of visualization software makes this task much easier.

Notes on patterns and insights

Record observations about what's working and what isn't.

Plan adjustments based on data

Document changes to your approach based on what the metrics reveal.

Your tracking system should take no more than 15 – 20 minutes per week to maintain. Complex systems become burdensome and get abandoned. Simple systems sustain long-term use.

Step 6: Create Your Accountability Structure

Finally, build the support structure that ensures follow-through when motivation wavers:

Select accountability partners

Identify 1 – 3 people who will:

- Know your plan in detail.
- Check in regularly on specific commitments.
- Provide both support and honest feedback.
- Hold you to your stated intentions.

Establish check-in schedule

Create regular times for:

- Daily personal review (5 minutes).
- Weekly detailed assessment (15 – 30 minutes).
- Partner check-ins (as appropriate).

Define outcomes

Decide what happens if you miss commitments:

- Positive outcomes for follow-through.
- Negative outcomes for avoidance.
- Mechanisms to get back on track after slips.

The key to effective accountability is specificity. "I'll check in with my friend" is too vague. "I'll send my friend a text every Friday with three actions completed and three planned for next week" creates clear expectations.

Real Results: The First 90 Days

After implementing this recovery plan, my situation improved steadily. The changes weren't dramatic day to day, but the cumulative effect over 90 days transformed my outlook and circumstances. Most importantly, I regained a sense of control. Even with many challenges still ahead, I no longer felt helpless. With each small win, I built confidence that recovery was possible.

The plan didn't eliminate all challenges, but it provided structure when everything felt chaotic. Having clear next steps kept me moving forward when I wasn't sure what to do next.

Chapter Summary

You now have an actionable recovery plan. This is the tool that transforms chaos into control, the fourth essential step in rebuilding after failure. You learned how most recovery attempts fail through reaction instead of action, attempting too much at once, lacking concrete steps, missing accountability, and neglecting emotional healing.

The five components of an effective recovery plan provide structure when life feels chaotic. Stabilization priorities stop panic and create space for strategic thinking. The 30/60/90-day framework breaks overwhelming challenges into manageable phases. Balancing quick wins with deep work maintains momentum while addressing root causes. Progress metrics make advancement visible when emotions might blind you to improvement. Accountability ensures follow-through when motivation inevitably wavers.

By following the process to create your personal recovery plan, you've transformed vague hopes into specific actions. This plan won't eliminate all challenges, but it provides direction when you feel lost, and control when circumstances seem overwhelming.

Most importantly, it moves you from reacting to responding, from crisis mode to strategic recovery.

This Week's Action Steps

1. Complete the Recovery Inventory for all five areas.
2. Identify your top three Stabilization Priorities.
3. Create your first 30-day plan with specific actions.
4. Select one quick win to accomplish this week.
5. Set up a simple tracking system for key metrics.
6. Identify at least one accountability partner and schedule your first check-in.

Key Takeaways

- Recovery requires both immediate stabilization and long-term rebuilding.
- Breaking your plan into 30-day phases prevents overwhelm and allows for adjustment.
- Tracking specific metrics makes progress visible when emotions cloud perception.
- Without accountability, even the best plans fail when motivation wavers.

Reflection Question

Which component of the recovery plan will be most challenging for you to implement?

Once identified, what specific support could help you overcome that challenge?

In the next chapter, you'll explore the fifth essential step in recovery: building a support network that provides both practical assistance and emotional sustenance during your rebuilding process.

You can't do this alone. Let's build your support team. A great plan is worthless without the right people to help you execute it. In the next chapter, you'll assemble your personal board of directors.

A Note About Community"

The exercises in this chapter work. I used them myself. But they work better when you're surrounded by people doing them with you. That's why I'm building The Resilience Protocol Community—a place where entrepreneurs support each other through recovery. Learn more at www.thecomebackguide.com.

Chapter 6:
Build a Support Network

The Power of Connection

My 3D printing business was failing. Debt had piled up. Cash reserves were gone. I felt completely isolated. For weeks, I avoided calls from friends and family, made excuses to skip gatherings, and hid the truth from my employee and my wife. I thought I needed to solve everything on my own.

The weight became too much that September evening in 2023. I walked through my front door, my wife standing there. Unable to hold back the tears, she asked, "What's going on?"

The question broke the dam. Everything poured out: the mounting debt, the failed product launches, the declining client base, the sleepless nights. I expected disappointment or anger. Instead, she sat next to me, listened without judgment, and asked questions about what closing the business would look like.

"Closing your business isn't the end," she said. "Keeping it open would be."

That conversation marked my first step toward recovery. The simple act of sharing my struggle lightened the burden. I wasn't alone anymore.

This pattern of isolation followed by connection repeated throughout my recovery. When I finally contacted a bankruptcy attorney, I discovered he had helped a lot of business owners through similar situations. When I joined a business networking group, I met others who understood exactly what I was experiencing. When I opened up to a close friend about my failure, he shared his career setbacks I'd never known about.

Each connection showed me something crucial: nobody recovers from failure alone. The support of others doesn't make recovery easier; it makes recovery possible.

Here's what I learned while recovering: the framework matters, but the people around you matter more. You can have the perfect plan and still give up when doubt creeps in at 2am. You can know exactly what to do and still freeze when fear takes over. You can understand your patterns and still repeat them without someone to call you out.

That's why I'm building The Resilience Protocol Community; a place where entrepreneurs who've experienced failure can support each other through recovery. Weekly coaching calls where we work through challenges together. A private forum where you can ask questions without judgment. Accountability partnerships that keep you moving forward on days when quitting feels easier.

The community launches soon after this book is published. If you want to be among the first members, go to www.thecomebackguide.com and add your name to the early access list. Founding members get special pricing and lifetime access to all future resources.

Recovery happens faster when you're surrounded by people who understand where you've been and where you're going.

Why We Face Failure Alone

Most of us try to handle business failure or career setbacks alone. This instinct makes recovery harder and longer than necessary.

When my business began failing, I withdrew from nearly everyone. This isolation wasn't random. It came from specific fears and misconceptions:

Fear of judgment: I worried others would see me as incompetent or a loser. I imagined conversations where people would say, "His business failed because he didn't know what he was doing." This fear kept me from reaching out to friends and fellow entrepreneurs who could have helped.

Shame about mistakes: I felt ashamed of my financial choices. I had taken loans for the wrong reasons. I had ignored warning signs. This shame made me hide problems even from my partner until the situation became desperate.

Illusion of self-reliance: It was always my belief that successful people solve their own problems. I saw asking for help as a last resort. This belief kept me from discussing the problems with mentors or advisors when small problems could have been addressed.

Protection of professional image: My ego wanted to maintain an image of success. I worried clients would leave if they knew about financial troubles. This concern prevented me from having honest conversations that might have created new opportunities and gave me options.

Misunderstanding of failure: I viewed failure as deeply personal, rather than a part of being a business owner. This perspective made me hide my situation instead of learning from others who had overcome similar challenges.

This isolation cost me. There were missed opportunities for early intervention. I tried to do everything alone when support was available. I made decisions without critical input that might have changed outcomes.

The myth of the "lone wolf" entrepreneur creates a dangerous trap. We celebrate stories of solo success while hiding the reality that behind every successful person stands a network of support.

The Cost of Isolation

Facing business failure alone creates specific problems:

- **Decision quality declines:** When stressed and isolated, your decision making suffers. During my business crisis, I made hasty choices without getting outside perspective. I continued spending on new equipment and paying old debt with new debt when sales were down. A mentor would have questioned these decisions.
- **Perspective narrows:** Isolation limits your viewpoint. I became fixated on short-term cash flow while ignoring

longer-term strategy. Others could have helped me see beyond immediate crises.
- **Physical health suffers:** Isolation increases stress, which affects physical health. My blood pressure rose. I gained weight. I suffered persistent neck pain. This physical toll made recovery harder.
- **Mental health deteriorates:** Facing failure alone increases risk of anxiety and depression. I experienced panic attacks when checking bank accounts. My sleep became disrupted by constant worry. These mental health challenges clouded my judgment.
- **Recovery takes longer:** Without support, you waste time reinventing solutions others have already discovered. I spent months trying to save my business when others with experience could have helped me recognize earlier that it was time to close.

Looking back, I see how my isolation became a self-reinforcing cycle. The worse I felt, the more I withdrew. The more I withdrew, the fewer resources I had to cope with my situation.

Breaking this cycle required conscious effort to build connections specifically designed to support recovery.

Quiz: Your Support Network Audit

Rate yourself on these statements from 1 (not at all) to 5 (completely):

1. ___**I can identify at least one person who fits each key support role (confidant, mentor, cheerleader, truth-teller, professional helper).** This measures whether you have a complete support team. Many people have some support but lack specific roles, leaving gaps where specific help is needed.
2. ___**I feel comfortable asking for help when I need it.** This gauges your ability to reach out during difficult times. After failure, many people struggle with vulnerability and asking for support, preferring to suffer alone.
3. ___**I have regular check-ins with supportive people in my life.** This evaluates whether you maintain ongoing connections rather than only reaching out during crises. Consistent relationships provide better support than emergency-only contacts.
4. ___**I know where to find professional help for specific challenges I'm facing.** This assesses your awareness of available resources. Knowing how to access therapists, career counselors, financial advisors, or other professionals is crucial during recovery.
5. ___**I recognize when I need support before reaching a crisis point.** This measures your self-awareness about support needs. People who can identify when they're struggling early get help before problems become overwhelming.

Calculate your score:_____

What Your Score Means:

- **5 – 10:** Building a support network is a critical priority for your recovery. You're likely facing challenges alone that would be easier with help.
- **11 – 15:** You have some support structures, but significant gaps remain. Focus on strengthening existing relationships and filling missing roles.
- **16 – 20:** You have a solid foundation of support. Work on deepening these relationships and maintaining regular connections.
- **21 – 25:** You have strong support-seeking skills and a robust network. Use this chapter to fine-tune your approach and help others build their networks.

My initial score? Only 12. While I had a network of professional contacts, friends and family, they were not part of my recovery plan. Once I began to reach out and make them a part of my recovery plan, my score went up to 19. There's still work to be done, but the added support has made a great deal of difference.

Building Your Recovery Team

No single person can provide all the support you need. Different challenges require different types of support.

Through my recovery, I discovered five essential roles that create a complete support network. This doesn't mean you need five different people for your support network. You might find multiple roles in one person, or you may need several people to fill a single role.

1. The Confidant: Your Safe Space

The confidant is someone you can tell everything without fear of judgment. This person creates space for your raw emotions and uncensored thoughts.

My wife became my primary confidant. After months of hiding my business problems, I finally shared everything. Instead of judging me, she listened with compassion. She didn't try to fix everything; she simply allowed me to be honest about my situation.

Your confidant will help you process emotions that might otherwise block progress. They might be a partner, close friend, or a family member. What matters is their ability to listen without judgement and without immediately trying to provide you with solutions.

When choosing a confidant, look for someone who:

- Maintains confidentiality.
- Listens more than they speak.
- Accepts emotions without trying to "fix" them.
- Has no direct stake in your business decisions.
- Creates a safe space free from judgment.

2. The Mentor: Your Guide

The mentor has walked a similar path and can share from experience. This person provides practical advice based on their own successes and failures.

After deciding to close my business, I was accepted into an entrepreneurship program. Though I was no longer focused on growing my company, the mentors allowed me to stay and helped guide my transition. While they were helping me figure out what came next, their practical advice about handling creditors, legal considerations, and personal recovery proved invaluable.

Your mentor might be a former boss, business owner in your network, or someone found through formal mentoring programs. What matters is their relevant experience and willingness to share honestly about both successes and failures.

When seeking a mentor, look for someone who:

- Has experience relevant to your situation.
- Speaks candidly about their own failures.
- Asks good questions rather than just giving answers.
- Challenges your thinking constructively.
- Balances empathy with practical guidance.

3. The Cheerleader: Your Encourager

The cheerleader reminds you of your strengths when you've forgotten them. This person helps rebuild your confidence after it's been shaken by failure.

A friend I'd known for years helped me get a contract job when I needed income. His confidence in my skills came when my own confidence was at its lowest. "I know this is in your wheelhouse," he said. This simple vote of confidence helped me see I still had value to offer despite my business failure.

Your cheerleader might be a friend, colleague, or family member. What matters is their genuine belief in your capabilities and their willingness to express that belief when you need it most.

When finding a cheerleader, look for someone who:

- Notices and names your specific strengths.
- Provides encouragement based on reality, not empty praise.
- Reminds you of past successes during difficult times.
- Helps you recognize progress you might overlook.

- Maintains optimism without denying challenges.

4. The Truth-Teller: Your Reality Check

The truth-teller provides honest feedback, even when it's uncomfortable. This person helps you avoid self-deception while forcing you to see blind spots and hard-to-face truths.

When planning my next venture, a good friend pointed out that my new plan repeated many patterns that led to my previous failure. This uncomfortable conversation saved me from making the same mistakes again. While it wasn't easy to hear, his honesty helped me create a more sustainable approach.

Your truth-teller might be a business partner, trusted colleague, or straight-talking friend. What matters is their willingness to say what needs to be said, even when it's difficult.

When seeking a truth-teller, look for someone who:

- Cares enough to be honest.
- Balances candor with compassion.
- Has good judgment and perspective.
- Isn't afraid of difficult conversations.
- Focuses on facts rather than emotions.

5. The Professional Helper: Your Expert Support

The professional helper provides specialized expertise for specific challenges. This person brings skills and knowledge beyond what friends or family can offer.

During my recovery, three professional helpers played crucial roles:

- A bankruptcy attorney, who guided me through legal processes.
- A therapist, who helped me develop tools for managing anxiety.
- A doctor, who addressed the physical impacts of chronic stress.

Your professional helpers will depend on your specific situation. They might include financial advisors, career counselors, or business consultants. What matters is their professional expertise in areas where you need specialized support.

When choosing professional helpers, look for:

- Relevant credentials and experience.
- Experience with situations similar to yours.
- A communication style that works for you.
- An approach that balances empathy with expertise.
- A clear explanation of their processes and fees.

Creating Your Support Strategy

Building an effective support network requires intention. Here's how to create your support strategy:

1. Assess Your Current Support

Begin by evaluating your existing relationships. Many people already have potential support team members but haven't utilized these connections effectively.

Make a list of people in your life in these categories:

- Family members.
- Close friends.
- Professional colleagues.
- Industry contacts.
- Former classmates or teachers.
- Community connections.

For each person, note:

- How close is your relationship?
- What support role could they potentially fill?
- How comfortable would you feel discussing your situation with them?
- What unique perspective or experience do they offer?

This assessment revealed surprising resources in my own network. A former colleague had gone through a business closure I hadn't known about. A family member had experience relevant to my situation. These connections were available but untapped because I hadn't been open about my needs.

2. Identify Support Gaps

Next, determine where your support network needs strengthening.

Ask yourself:

- Which of the five support roles are currently unfilled?
- In what areas do I feel most isolated or unsupported?
- What specific knowledge or expertise would help my situation?
- Which emotions or challenges am I having trouble handling alone?

My assessment showed I had a strong confidant (my wife) but lacked a mentor with relevant business failure experience. I also needed professional help with the legal and financial aspects of closing my business.

3. Expand Your Network Strategically

Once you've identified gaps, take specific steps to build connections where needed.

Strategies that helped me include:

- **Join structured groups:** I joined local business networking groups, which helped. But here's what made the real difference: connecting with entrepreneurs who'd experienced the same failure I had. These conversations happen in specialized recovery communities where everyone understands the shame, the sleepless nights, and the identity crisis.
  The Resilience Protocol Community is made to bring together entrepreneurs at every stage of recovery. You'll

meet people one week ahead of you (showing you it gets better) and people six months ahead (proving recovery is real). This matters because general networking groups offer encouragement, while recovery communities offer understanding.

Discover more at **www.thecomebackguide.com**.

- **Use existing connections as bridges:** I asked trusted friends if they knew anyone who had experienced business closure. This led to several valuable connections I wouldn't have made otherwise.
- **Be specific about needs:** Rather than vaguely asking for "help," I learned to request specific types of support: "Could you review my resume?" "Would you be willing to share how you handled closing your business?" Specific requests made it easier for others to assist.
- **Give before you take:** I looked for ways to provide value to potential mentors and advisors. Offering something, even expressing sincere interest in their experience, made these relationships more balanced.
- **Utilize professional associations:** Industry groups often have resources for members facing challenges. My local entrepreneurs' association connected me with a mentor who specialized in business transitions.

4. Establish Support Routines

Regular connection prevents isolation from returning during your recovery process.

Support routines that helped me:

- **Morning coffee with my wife:** We created "Couch Time," a simple daily ritual of sitting together with coffee before starting our day. This brief connection helped me process feelings and plan next steps.
- **Regular check-ins with a mentor:** A regularly scheduled call kept me accountable and provided guidance without requiring a major time commitment from either of us.

- **Monthly professional group meetings:** Regular attendance at a business networking group provided perspective and reminded me I wasn't alone in my challenges.
- **Therapy appointments:** Consistent sessions with my therapist gave me space to work through deeper issues related to identity and self-worth after business failure.

These routines created a scaffold of support that sustained me through the ups and downs of recovery.

5. Learn to Ask and Receive

Many of us struggle more with receiving help than with offering it. Learning to ask for and accept support is a skill that requires practice.

Approaches that helped me overcome resistance to seeking help:

- **Start small:** I began by asking for specific, limited forms of support, rather than sharing my entire situation at once. This built my comfort with vulnerability gradually.
- **Practice the words:** I rehearsed asking for help, practicing speaking out loud sentences like, "I'm going through a difficult business situation and could use your perspective."
- **Focus on mutual benefit:** I recognized that sharing my experience might help others with their challenges. This shifted my perspective from "burdening others" to "creating mutual support."
- **Accept help graciously:** I learned to respond to offers of help with, "Thank you, I appreciate that," rather than, "I'm fine," or "Don't worry about me."
- **Recognize the gift of trust:** I came to understand that asking for help honors the relationship by demonstrating trust in the other person.

The Art of Asking for Help

Many people struggle with asking for help. These approaches make the process easier:

Be Specific About Needs

Instead of vague requests, clearly state what would be helpful.
Vague: "I'm having a hard time with my business situation."
Specific: "I'd appreciate 30 minutes to get your perspective on organizing a business closure."

Frame as Time-Limited Support

People are more likely to help when they understand the time commitment.
Open-ended: "I need help with my business transition."
Time-limited: "Would you be willing to review my business plan once a month for the next three months as I get my new business set up?"

Offer Reciprocity

Show willingness to provide value in return.
One-sided: "Can you introduce me to potential clients?"
Reciprocal: "I'd like to learn how you built your client base. I'm happy to share my experience with AI implementation in return."

Acknowledge Their Expertise

People respond to recognition of their specific knowledge or experience.
Generic: "I need business advice."
Acknowledging: "Your experience turning around your company would be particularly helpful as I navigate my situation."

Express Genuine Appreciation

Thank people specifically for their help and its impact.
General: "Thanks for your help."

Specific: "Your advice about how to plan my closure saved me significant stress and money. I'm truly grateful for your guidance."

Real Results:
How My Support Network Made Recovery Possible

Building a support network transformed my recovery journey in specific ways:

When I struggled with overwhelming shame about business failure, regular conversations with my confidant (my wife) provided emotional safety to process these feelings. Over time, these conversations helped me separate my identity from my business outcomes.

When I faced complex bankruptcy decisions, my attorney, who understood the process, provided practical guidance that saved me time and reduced my legal costs. His experience helped me avoid common pitfalls and instead, allowed me to make informed choices during a confusing process.

When my confidence was shattered, my cheerleader reminded me of skills and strengths that remained valuable. This encouragement led directly to contract work that provided income during my transition period.

When I began planning a new venture, my truth-teller pointed out that I was repeating old patterns. This frank feedback helped me create a more sustainable business model aligned with my values and skills.

When anxiety threatened my recovery, my professional helper (therapist) provided specific tools for managing stress. These techniques improved both my mental wellbeing and decision-making ability during a challenging time.

The combined effect of this support network wasn't emotional comfort alone. It produced tangible outcomes that accelerated my recovery and created a foundation for my next chapter.

Chapter Summary

You discovered how building a strategic support network helps in recovery from business failure or career setbacks. Examined why many people face failure alone and the high costs of isolation during challenging times.

You identified five essential support roles that create a complete recovery team: the confidant who provides emotional safety, the mentor who offers experienced guidance, the cheerleader who builds confidence, the truth-teller who provides honest feedback, and the professional helper who contributes specialized expertise.

You've identified specific steps for creating your support strategy: assessing current support, identifying gaps, expanding your network strategically, establishing support routines, and learning to ask for and receive help effectively.

Remember that seeking support isn't a sign of weakness, but a strategic approach to recovery. The strongest people aren't those who handle everything alone—they're those who know how to build and utilize the right support network for each challenge they face.

This Week's Action Steps

1. Complete the Support Network Assessment exercise to map your current support.
2. Identify your biggest support gap and list three potential people who could fill this role.
3. Practice asking for help by making one specific request to someone in your network.
4. Schedule a regular check-in with one key supporter for the next month.

5. Send a note of appreciation to someone who has supported you during your challenge.

Key Takeaways

- Nobody recovers from failure alone; connection is essential to the process.
- Different challenges require different types of support from various people.
- Building an effective support network requires intention and specific actions.
- Learning to ask for and receive help is a skill that can be developed with practice.
- The right support network creates both emotional comfort and practical benefits.

Reflection Question

Which support role, if filled or strengthened, would make the biggest difference in your recovery right now?

Remember: Seeking support isn't weakness—it's the strategic approach that successful people use to navigate challenges more effectively.

Now that you've been through each of the 5 steps, it's time to put it all together and move forward.

Part III: The New Beginning

Chapter 7: Moving Forward with Confidence

The Journey So Far

Congratulations! You've now walked through all five steps of **The Resilience Protocol**. Now that your recovery journey is well under way, I thank you for being a part of mine.

The day the company closed felt like an ending. My identity as a business owner, my daily purpose, my sense of accomplishment, all vanished. Packing the last box and taking a final look around, the knot in my stomach had become a constant companion by then. The business represented years of my life, dreams, sweat, pride, and, ultimately, painful lessons. I didn't know what came next. The future looked blank and frightening.

Maybe you're at this point now. Or maybe you're still in the middle of closing your business or recovering from job loss. You might be wondering if you'll ever feel confident again. If you'll ever stop feeling like a failure. If you'll ever find purpose and direction after such a setback.

I can tell you from experience—this is *not* the end of your story. While it is the end of one chapter, it's also the beginning of a new one.

The journey you've taken through this book parallels my own recovery path. From the raw honesty of self-assessment to the gradual rebuilding of resilience. From setting new goals to creating actionable plans. From isolation to building a network of support. Each step moved me from devastation toward a new beginning.

Today, I stand in a different place than I could have imagined during those dark days. The business failure that once defined me has become one of my greatest learning experiences. The lessons it taught have proven more valuable than the money I lost. The person who emerged from that failure is stronger, wiser, and—paradoxically—more successful than before, though my definition of success has fundamentally changed.

What You've Learned

Take a moment to review what you've discovered on this journey.

Step 1: Conduct an Honest Self-Assessment

You learned to evaluate four key areas of your life:

- Financial reality: looking at the numbers objectively.
- Skills inventory: identifying your strengths and gaps.
- Relationship patterns: seeing how connections affect outcomes.
- Values alignment: ensuring your actions match what matters most.

This foundation of self-knowledge prevents you from carrying old patterns into new ventures. It helps you start fresh, with clear understanding, rather than wishful thinking.

Step 2: Develop a Resilient Mindset

You discovered the four pillars of mental resilience:

- Identity separation: knowing you are not your failure
- Explanatory style: how you tell the story of what happened
- Emotional regulation: managing feelings without being controlled by them
- Growth perspective: finding value in difficult experiences

These mental tools help you bounce back faster from setbacks and maintain mental balance during times of uncertainty.

Step 3: Set Clear, Achievable Goals

You learned the SMART+ framework for effective goal setting:

- Specific goals that provide clear direction
- Measurable progress you can track
- Achievable targets that build confidence
- Relevant objectives aligned with your journey
- Time-bound deadlines that create momentum
- Plus values: alignment and adaptability

This structured approach transforms vague hopes into concrete, forward steps.

Step 4: Create an Actionable Recovery Plan

You built a comprehensive plan with five essential components:

- Stabilization priorities that stop further damage
- A 30/60/90-day framework that creates manageable phases
- Balance between quick wins and deeper progress
- Progress metrics that make advancement visible
- Accountability structures that ensure follow-through

This plan converts overwhelming challenges into sequential tasks you can handle one at a time.

Step 5: Build a Support Network

You identified the five roles needed in your recovery team:

- The confidant, who provides emotional safety

- The mentor, who offers experienced guidance
- The cheerleader, who builds confidence
- The truth-teller, who provides honest feedback
- The professional helper, who contributes specialized expertise

This network prevents isolation and provides both practical help and emotional support when you need it most.

Together, these five tips create a roadmap for navigating from failure to a new beginning. But knowing the path is only the first step. Walking it requires persistence, courage, and faith in your ability to rebuild.

The Reality of Recovery

Let me be completely honest about what recovery looks like. It's not a straight line upward. It's not a miraculous transformation. It's not a single "aha" moment that suddenly makes everything better.

Real recovery looks more like this:

You'll have days when you feel strong and purposeful, followed by days when doubt returns. You'll make progress in one area while struggling in another. You'll experience small victories alongside continuing challenges. Some days, you'll feel proud of how far you've come; other days, you'll feel frustrated by how far you still need to go.

This uneven progress is normal. It doesn't mean you're failing at recovery. It means you're human.

My own recovery journey had many setbacks:

- Financial constraints that limited options
- Moments of doubt about my new direction
- Days when the past felt more real than the future

What's kept me moving forward isn't perfection. It's persistence. On good days, I made progress. On bad days, I simply didn't quit. Over time, the good days began to outnumber the bad. The steps forward exceeded the steps back. Momentum built slowly but steadily.

Your recovery timeline will be unique to you. It depends on many factors: the nature of your setback, your financial situation, your support system, your emotional resilience, external market conditions. Don't measure your progress against someone else's timeline or expect instantaneous results.

What matters isn't how quickly you recover, but that you keep moving in the right direction, even when that movement feels painfully slow.

Common Obstacles and How to Overcome Them

During your recovery journey, you'll likely encounter several common obstacles. Recognizing them helps you navigate around them, rather than being stopped by them.

1. The Comparison Trap

You might find yourself comparing your current situation to:

- Where you were before failure.
- Where you "should" be by now.
- Where others in your field are.
- Where you would be if you hadn't failed.

These comparisons fuel negative emotions without providing useful guidance. When you catch yourself making them, redirect your attention to:

- Progress from your lowest point.
- Realistic expectations for your situation.
- Your own unique path.
- Lessons you've gained that others might not have.

2. Identity Aftershocks

Even after the intellectual acceptance of your changed circumstances, your ego may struggle to catch up. You might instinctively reach for a business card you no longer have. And when introducing yourself without your former title, you may feel diminished.

These identity aftershocks can be managed by:

- Creating new self-descriptions that feel authentic.
- Focusing on enduring aspects of your identity.
- Finding meaning in new roles and activities.
- Allowing yourself to grieve the loss while embracing new possibilities.

3. Financial Pressure

Practical financial concerns can overshadow emotional and psychological recovery. Bills don't stop coming because you're rebuilding your life.

Manage financial pressure through:

- Creating a bare-minimum budget for essential needs.
- Finding temporary income sources while pursuing longer-term goals.
- Making arrangements with creditors when possible.
- Reminding yourself that financial recovery takes time.

4. Well-Meaning But Unhelpful People

Friends and family who haven't experienced similar setbacks may offer advice that feels disconnected from your reality. They might say things like:

- "Just start another business!"
- "At least you tried!"
- "Everything happens for a reason!"

Handle these situations by:

- Recognizing the good intentions behind the unhelpful comments.
- Identifying which people truly understand your experience.
- Setting boundaries around recovery conversations.
- Educating others about what support looks like for you.

5. Recovery Fatigue

The constant effort of rebuilding can become exhausting. You might experience periods of burnout where you simply feel tired of trying.

Combat recovery fatigue through:

- Building rest and renewal into your recovery plan.
- Celebrating small victories to maintain momentum.
- Adjusting expectations during particularly difficult periods.
- Leaning on your support network when your energy lags.

Each of these obstacles is normal and surmountable. Anticipating them reduces their power to derail your progress.

Creating Your New Chapter

Recovery isn't about getting back to where you were. It's about creating something new, often something better than what existed before.

For me, my initial focus was on what I'd lost. But as my recovery progressed, my perspective shifted toward what I could create next. This creative mindset transformed my focus from simply healing wounds to building something valuable from my experience.

Here's how to approach creating your new chapter:

Draw from All You've Learned

Your failure contains valuable information about:

- What works for you and what doesn't.
- Your true strengths and weaknesses.
- What truly matters to you.
- How you respond under pressure.

Use this self-knowledge to create a more aligned path forward. I discovered through my business failure that I valued creative work, helping others, and work-life balance more than business growth or status. This insight shaped my next chapter.

Look for Unexpected Opportunities

Failure often creates openings that weren't visible before:

- Skills developed through necessity during crisis.
- Connections made during the recovery process.
- Perspectives gained from the experience.
- Problems you're now uniquely positioned to solve.

My own failure led me to discover talents for writing and creative thinking that I might never have explored otherwise. This very book you're reading exists because of a door that opened after another closed.

Design with Intention

Rather than rushing toward the first available opportunity, take time to design your next chapter intentionally:

- What elements must be present for you to thrive?
- What boundaries will protect you from past patterns?
- What values will guide your decisions?
- What definition of success will drive your efforts?

I created a written "next chapter design" with non-negotiable elements (work that utilized my creativity, income sufficient for financial security, time for relationships) and clear boundaries (no business debt, structured work hours, regular financial reviews).

Start Small, but Start

Your next chapter doesn't need to begin with grand gestures. Small, concrete steps create momentum toward larger changes:

- Take a class in an area that interests you.
- Have coffee with someone in a field you're exploring.
- Create a simple project that uses your skills in new ways.
- Volunteer where you can add value while learning.

My first step was simply writing about my experience for myself. This small action eventually led to conversations, then networking, and finally to the book you're reading now. The path revealed itself one step at a time.

How Success Looks Now

A profound change from my failure experience wasn't external but internal, a complete redefinition of what success means.

Before my business failed, success looked like:

- Growing revenue.
- An expanding business.
- Industry recognition.
- Status in my community.
- External validation.

These markers drove my decisions, often at the cost of my health, relationships, and inner peace. They made me vulnerable to failure because they existed largely outside my control.

Today, success looks different:

- Financial sufficiency, rather than wealth.
- Meaningful work, rather than impressive titles.
- Strong relationships, rather than transactional ones.
- Personal wellbeing, rather than professional status.
- Internal fulfillment, rather than external validation.

This definition serves me better because:

- It's largely within my control.
- It supports rather than damages my health.
- It creates sustainable satisfaction.
- It aligns with my true values.
- It's harder to lose in economic downturns.

The irony? I'm more "successful" with this new definition than I was with the old one. My work reaches more people. My relationships are more fulfilling. My professional reputation continues to grow. But these outcomes aren't the point; they're byproducts of pursuing what truly matters.

I invite you to reconsider what success means for *you*. Not what society, your industry, or even your past self defined as success. Consider what would bring genuine fulfillment and meaning in your next chapter.

A New Definition of Success

I used to define success by external markers—revenue growth, industry recognition, impressive clients. My ego was wrapped up in achievements I could show off at networking events. When people asked how business was, I'd talk about numbers, never whether I was happy.

The collapse of my company stripped all that away. Suddenly, those external markers were gone. At first, this felt like having my identity erased. Who was I without it? What could I point to as evidence of my worth? This identity crisis was painful but necessary. It forced me to rebuild my definition of success from the ground up.

Now, I understand that success looks like:

- Strong relationships where I'm fully present.
- Good physical and mental health.
- Helping others by sharing what I've learned.

- Learning from challenges instead of being defeated by them.
- Time for hobbies and interests outside work.
- The ability to say "no" to opportunities that don't align with my values.

The shift wasn't easy. Our culture constantly reinforces the old definition of success—bigger, more, faster. Breaking free from that mindset requires effort. I started by noticing moments of joy each day that had nothing to do with work or achievement. A conversation with my wife over morning coffee. Helping a friend solve a problem. Learning something new simply for the pleasure of learning.

I began asking different questions. Instead of "How can I make more money?", I asked, "How can I create more value for others?" Instead of "How can I look successful?", I asked, "What actually makes me feel fulfilled?", Instead of "What will impress others?", I asked, "What will I be glad I did when I look back on my life?"

This change took months of thinking, talking with loved ones, and honestly asking myself what made me happy. I had to confront some uncomfortable truths. I had been chasing success partly to impress people whose opinions didn't matter to me. I had been working in ways that damaged my health because I thought that's what successful people did. I had been postponing joy for some future date when I'd finally "made it."

The strange part? I'm happier now with this new definition than I was when chasing the old one. There's freedom in no longer feeling like I must impress everyone. There's peace in knowing my worth isn't tied to my last quarter's performance. And there's genuine fulfillment in building a life around what truly matters, rather than what merely looks good.

What's your definition of success? Is it truly yours, or have you inherited it from others? What would change in your life if you measured success by fulfillment rather than achievement?

Your Recovery Toolkit

Throughout this book, you've gathered specific tools for your recovery journey. Let's summarize them here for easy reference:

Self-Assessment Tools

- The four-part assessment framework (financial, skills, relationships, values)
- Personal timeline exercise
- Pattern recognition questions
- Self-assessment quiz
- Values/actions alignment check

Resilience Tools

- Identity separation exercise
- Thought reframing practice
- Emotional regulation techniques
- Growth perspective questions
- Daily resilience habits
- Emergency resilience protocol

Goal-Setting Tools

- SMART+ goal framework
- Vision-to-tasks hierarchy
- Reality alignment checklist
- Weekly goal tracker
- Values-goals connection map

Planning Tools

- Recovery inventory template
- Stabilization priorities worksheet
- 30/60/90-day planning framework
- Progress metrics dashboard
- Accountability structure design

Support Network Tools

- Support role identification guide
- Network gap assessment
- Connection strategy template
- Support routine scheduler
- Help-asking scripts

These tools remain available whenever you need them. You might use some daily during early recovery, then less frequently as you stabilize. Others might become regular practices you carry forward into your new chapter.

The toolkit is adaptable to your unique situation. Use what works for you, modify what needs adjustment, and add new tools as you discover them. Find out more about the recovery toolkit at **www.thecomebackguide.com**

Your Next Steps

So, where do you go from here?
How do you move from reading about recovery to living it?
Here's a simple 7-day plan to build momentum:

Day 1: Take a Personal Inventory

Go to **www.thecomebackguide.com**. And join the community.

Day 2: Create Your Resilience Routine

Select one daily practice that will strengthen your mental foundation.

Day 3: Set Your First Recovery Goal

Choose one short-term goal using the SMART+ framework.

Day 4: Identify Your Support Team

List potential people for each of the five support roles.

Day 5: Make Your First Outreach

Contact one person from your support list with a specific request.

Day 6: Design Your First Week's Plan

Create a specific daily action plan for the coming week.

Day 7: Establish Your Progress Tracking

Set up a simple system to monitor your forward movement.
This first week starts your recovery engine. From there, expand gradually:

- Add more detailed assessments in areas that need attention.
- Develop additional goals as you gain clarity.
- Build your full support network.
- Create longer-term planning horizons as you progress.
- Adjust your approach based on what works for you.

Remember that action creates clarity. You don't need perfect understanding before you begin. Each step you take will reveal more about your path forward.

My Journey Continues

I want to share a bit about where I am as of completing this book.

As this book got started, a little over 1 year since closing, my life looks nothing like I would have predicted during those dark days:

- I'm building a new business combining my writing and teaching based on what I've learned. It's both training and a community to help others recover from their business failure and move on.

    www.thecomebackguide.com

- I maintain a healthy relationship with work, rather than letting it consume my identity.

- My financial situation has stabilized through mindful planning and clear priorities.

- My relationships have deepened through authentic connection rather than surface-level networking.

- My physical and mental health have improved dramatically with sustainable habits and regular exercise.
- My sense of purpose comes from helping others navigate challenges similar to what I faced.

Most importantly, I've made peace with my failure. It no longer defines me. It's simply one chapter in a longer story; a chapter that contained valuable lessons that needed to be learned.

This doesn't mean everything is perfect. There are still daily challenges. Mistakes made. And days when old doubts resurface. But these moments no longer derail progress like they once did. The tools I've shared with you in this book have now become second nature, helping me respond to difficulties with resilience and clarity.

Your journey will look different from mine. Your next chapter will reflect your unique skills, values, circumstances, and choices. I'm confident that if you apply these principles, you'll find your way forward, as I found mine.

This Week's Action Steps

1. Complete a brief written reflection on what you've learned from this book.
2. Select the one tip that resonates most strongly and commit to implementing it fully.
3. Share one insight from your journey with someone who might benefit.
4. Create a simple ritual to mark your transition from recovery to rebuilding.
5. Schedule a 30-day check-in with yourself to assess your progress.

Key Takeaways

- Recovery isn't linear. Expect both progress and setbacks as part of the normal process.
- Your next chapter can be more aligned with your true values than what came before.
- Success redefined according to your terms creates more sustainable fulfillment.
- Small, consistent actions create momentum toward larger transformation.
- Your response to failure, not failure itself, determines your future.

A Final Word of Encouragement

If you take only one thing from this book, let it be this: Failure is not the end of your story. It's one step along the path that will lead you to valuable lessons and a better future.

The business that fails, the job that's lost, the career that derails—these are events, not identities. They are experiences, not definitions. They are moments in time, not permanent conditions.

You are not your failure.

You are your response to failure. You are your resilience in difficult times. You are your willingness to learn and grow. You are your courage to begin again.

Every successful person has failed. Many have failed spectacularly, and more than once. What separates them from those permanently defined by failure is simply this: they kept going. They used what they learned. They built something new from the ruins of the old.

You can do the same.

The path defined in this book works. I know because I've walked it. Others have walked it. The principles of honest self-assessment, resilient thinking, clear goal setting, strategic planning, and supportive connection have guided countless people from failure to new beginnings.

Now, it's your turn to take action.

You've already taken the first step by reading this book. Don't let it be the last. Choose one small action today that moves you forward. Then another tomorrow. Build momentum, one decision at a time.

There will be difficult days ahead. Days when doubt creeps back in. Days when progress is slow. Days when the past feels more real than the future. On those days, return to the tools and principles you've learned. Lean on your support network.

Remember how far you've already come. And join our community to find supportive people who understand what you have been through.

And keep going.

Because your story isn't over. This difficult chapter, the one where everything fell apart, is just that: one chapter. You get to write what happens next.

I believe in your ability to recover, rebuild, and create something meaningful from what you've experienced. The very fact that you've engaged with this book shows your commitment to moving forward.

Take that commitment and transform it into action.

The Choice Point

Every entrepreneur who experiences failure reaches a moment where they must choose: face recovery alone or find their people. The ones who recover fastest make that choice early. They recognize that the framework in this book provides the map, but the community provides the fuel.

You've finished the book. The framework lives in these pages. The transformation happens when you apply it.

Here's What I Know About Recovery

The entrepreneurs who recover fastest share one thing: they refuse to face this alone. They find their people. They show up. They do the work together.

I recovered from business failure using the five steps you learned in this book. The framework worked. But what made recovery possible was the network I built; the people who understood my pain, held me accountable, and reminded me on dark days that this wasn't the end.

The Resilience Protocol Community

That's why I'm creating The Resilience Protocol Community. A place where entrepreneurs recovering from failure can:

- Attend weekly group coaching calls and work through the framework together
- Connect in a private forum with people who understand your experience
- Partner with accountability buddies who keep you moving forward
- Access extended resources, video training, and expert interviews

- Ask questions directly and get guidance when you're stuck

The community launches shortly after this book is published. If you want to be among the founding members, go to www.thecomebackguide.com and join the early access list.

Why Founding Members Matter

Founding members get special pricing locked in for life. You'll help shape what this community becomes. You'll be the entrepreneurs who prove that recovery is possible, showing others who come after you that they can rebuild too.

Your recovery story matters. The community needs your experience as much as you need theirs.

Your Next Step

Go to www.thecomebackguide.com and add your name to the early access list. You'll get an email when the community launches

Be among the first to join

Start building the support network that makes recovery inevitable

The Truth About Recovery

You can work through this framework alone. The steps are all here. Everything you need to know is in these chapters. But recovery goes faster when you're surrounded by people taking the same steps.

The entrepreneurs who thrive after failure find their people early. They build their support network before they feel ready. They show up even when it's uncomfortable.

That's what The Resilience Protocol Community offers—your people, your network, your tribe of entrepreneurs who refuse to let failure be the end of the story.

Take Action Now

- Visit www.thecomebackguide.com
- Sign up for early access

I'll see you when the community launches
Your comeback starts when you stop facing this alone

Steven

P.S. - Have questions about the community? Email me at stevens@thecomebackguide.com. I respond to every message personally."

Your next chapter awaits.

Go to
www.thecomebackguide.com
Take your first step today.

Acknowledgements

This book happened because I learned something important: recovering from failure requires other people. **Andrea Gaboriault**, my editor, did the bulk of the editing work, helping me sound coherent and organizing the book so it makes sense. **Constance G Burt** did a second pass on the editing and helped clean up the text even more, catching the details that would have driven readers crazy. **Scott Shwarts** pushed me to question my basic assumptions, asking things like, "Just a question, is 'success' really the goal?"; the kind of comment that stops you cold and makes you rethink everything. **Karl Davenport** who read the entire manuscript and gave me honest feedback that helped me see where the book worked and where it needed work. **Chris Hanson** who let me bounce ideas off him and talk through what was happening with the book and my life; sometimes, you just need someone who will listen. **April**, my wife, lived through every failure I describe in these pages. When I was still trying to save the business, she could see what I couldn't; that it was time to let go. Later, when I wondered if anyone would want to read about my mistakes, she pushed me to keep writing.

The **Asheville business community** wrapped their arms around me when my world fell apart. Instead of judgment or awkward silence, I found people who understood that business failure doesn't make you an outsider. It makes you part of the club. They showed me that we're all in this together, whether we're celebrating wins or picking up the pieces.

Maybe you picked up this book because your own world fell apart recently. Here's what everyone I just mentioned taught me: trying to rebuild alone is like trying to perform surgery on yourself. Get help. Accept it when people offer. Then, help someone else when you can.

About the Author

Steven Schain is the author of The Comeback Guide for Entrepreneurs and the creator of The Resilience Protocol. He knows what it feels like to watch everything you've built crumble around you because he's lived it. After successfully building and selling his first company, Spectralight Images, in 2016 following 18 years of growth, Steven thought he had entrepreneurship figured out. He was wrong.

His second venture, Spectra3D, brought him face-to-face with every entrepreneur's worst nightmare. The debt kept growing. Revenue kept shrinking. The stress was crushing him. By 2023, Steven had to make the hardest decision of his professional life to close the doors and file for bankruptcy. It felt like his career was over. Turns out, it was just getting started.

These days, Steven has turned that devastating experience into his life's work. With over 30 years in training and education, including creating educational content for major software companies, he now runs AI Performance Partners. His mission? Help business owners and professionals who are going through what he went through. Steven doesn't teach theory. He teaches what he experienced, the sleepless nights, the tough conversations, the step-by-step process of clawing your way back.

After rebuilding his own life, Steven created The Resilience Protocol Community to ensure other entrepreneurs don't have to face recovery alone. Through weekly coaching calls, private forum discussions, and accountability partnerships, he guides entrepreneurs through the same five-step system that transformed his own failure into his life's most meaningful work.

Steven lives in beautiful Western North Carolina with his amazing wife. They're proud of their four grown kids, all doing incredible things with their lives. When he's not coaching people through their comeback stories, you'll find Steven tinkering with 3D printing projects, teaching AI and 3D design, or exploring the mountains and music scene around Asheville. His philosophy is simple: Failure isn't your final chapter. It's the first line of your comeback story.

www.ingramcontent.com/pod-product-compliance
Lightning Source LLC
Chambersburg PA
CBHW022134080426
42734CB00006B/359